INTEGRITY
AND COMPROMISE

INTEGRITY
AND COMPROMISE

Problems of
Public and Private Conscience

EDITED BY

Robert M. MacIver

Essay Index Reprint Series

Originally published by
THE INSTITUTE for RELIGIOUS and SOCIAL STUDIES

BOOKS FOR LIBRARIES PRESS
FREEPORT, NEW YORK

Library of Congress Cataloging in Publication Data

Institute for Religious and Social Studies, Jewish
    Theological Seminary of America.
    Integrity and compromise; problems of public and
private conscience.

    (Essay index reprint series)
    Original ed. issued in series: Religion and civili-
zation series.
    "Series of luncheon addresses delivered ... during
the winter 1955-1956."
    Includes bibliographical references.
    1. Self-respect. 2. Compromise (Ethics)
I. MacIver, Robert Morrison, 1882-1970, ed. II. Title.
III. Series: Religion and civilization series.
[BJ1533.S3I5 1972]   170   74-167367
ISBN 0-8369-2656-0

PRINTED IN THE UNITED STATES OF AMERICA
BY
NEW WORLD BOOK MANUFACTURING CO., INC.
HALLANDALE, FLORIDA 33009

This volume contains the series of luncheon addresses delivered at The Institute for Religious and Social Studies of The Jewish Theological Seminary of America during the winter of 1955–1956. This year we have included a few of the discussions from the floor that are a feature of the luncheon series. It was felt that they would help to give the reader a better idea of the character of our meetings, especially since the discussions often elicit points of interest not dwelt on in the lectures themselves.

Each chapter in this volume represents solely the individual opinion of the author. Neither the Institute nor the editor assumes responsibility for the views expressed. We have been fortunate enough to enlist a group of authors each of whom has distinctive knowledge in his own field, and the Institute is indeed grateful for the generous way in which they have responded to its invitation.

This is a Jacob Ziskind Memorial publication.

CONTENTS

I

NECESSITY OF COMPROMISE

BY

FRANCIS BIDDLE

When I was asked to speak about the problems of compromise, I was uncertain what form my remarks might take. So I thought I could let the subject rest under a generality which would give me room to move in almost any direction.

The chairman's introduction that, having been Attorney General and a lawyer, I certainly knew what compromise meant, reminds me of what Judge Knox, the New York Federal District judge, said many years ago to a group of Philadelphians, in discussing the Fourth Amendment. His opening remark, that it was not necessary to talk to Philadelphians about the problem of self-incrimination, broke the ice, as it were.

I want to say something about the theory of compromise, the necessity of compromise, and what compromise is and what it is not. In looking over the other titles in this series, it seemed to me that they dealt with specific problems, and that perhaps it might have value in one's thinking about this, to pull together the types of compromise with which one is daily faced, and to evolve from them some philosophy or point of view.

Of course it is obvious to any American that our whole national life is built on compromise, and that the great institution, the American Constitution, from which we suck the strength of our public life, is in itself a series of compromises, great and small, the compromises between the states and the national government, between the central power and the power on the periphery; and between, to be realistic, the Southern interests of Southern planters and farmers and the shipping interests of New England.

It was interesting that, realizing the consequences of compromise on such profound national issues, the delegates to the Constitutional Convention held all their sessions in secret. Therefore the country did not realize until after it was all over that the delegates were, from the very beginning, doing something which they had absolutely no right to do, organizing a new constitution instead of amending the unworkable constitution of the Continental Congress which had bound them together before; and, secondly, carrying out the more specific compromises of which I have spoken. It was not until many years afterward that the discussions of the Convention were made public, and the public realized how bitter and how extreme the points of view were. It was not unnatural that when the Constitution came to the various states for ratification, the feeling, even though several months had elapsed, ran tremendously high, particularly in Pennsylvania, where there was actual violence. Some of the delegates did not want to hold a meeting to ratify. They were dragged out of bed by mobs and made to sit in their chairs and vote on it one way or the other. Probably the best debate was in the state of Virginia. But the great compromise finally went through.

I dwell on that, perhaps a little too much, because I want to contrast it with a somewhat different system and technique that we are using today. Burke in his great speech on conciliation with America said about compromise: "All government, indeed every human benefit and enjoyment, every virtue, and every prudent act is founded on compromise and barter." Barter has a nice eighteenth century sound about it. "We balance inconveniences"—and this is Burke's detestation of abstractions, speaking so specifically and concretely now, having first generalized—"we balance inconveniences, we give and take"—and this is the essence of what he said, and is important to remember today, particularly in the international field —"we give and take, we remit some rights that we may enjoy others."

The word "compromise" itself has caused a great deal of semantic difficulty. Nobody knows what it means. Like so many words coming down through the centuries, it takes on a different color in different periods. At present it seems to me to have a combination of the red and the yellow—the yellow as if there were something vicious or evil about any compromise; and the red, of course—we must never compromise with our enemies.

Before going further into the definition of compromise let me say what it is not. In the first place it is not, to use a phrase of Lord Morley from his famous essay on compromise, "an indolent acquiescence in error"; nor, indeed, does it suggest indifference. A man can be passionately involved in furthering the principle that he cares about, and yet, either from necessity or because the very compromise in the field with which he is dealing will perhaps some day further that principle, he works out a compromise. Turgot said, "I am a great enemy of indifference, a great friend of indulgence."

Another thing which is generally perhaps a little less understood is that bowing to the will of the majority is not really compromise in the true sense. Bowing to the will of the majority, to the vote of the people, to an act of the legislature, to a thing that has become law, even if you dislike it, that is really a method of setting up an umpire which you have agreed to abide by.

In the field of international law, to which I will refer later, there is no umpire, there is no congress, there is no law which really governs, except in special circumstances and then, usually, by consent. So that the problems of international compromise are entirely different from the problems of domestic compromise in a democracy where the technique of solving those problems by an umpire has already been worked out.

Reverting again to the domestic scene, it has often been said that there is never any substantial difference of opinion or of program between the two great parties in America. What, says a critic of American institutions, fundamentally is the difference between the Democrat and the Republican? They stand, really, for the same things; not, perhaps, when they are name-calling; not possibly, in the platforms; but in the ultimate choice there is no issue of principle or policy. Why have parties? Does this system create original leadership? Does it permit the kind of differences of opinion which a democracy should have?

I think that is largely a misunderstanding of the American government. It seems to me that what the mechanism of national, state, city, and local governments permits is the solving of difficulties and issues which are passionate and real; but solving them, on the whole, below the surface of elections, so that only a few of the issues come up in the long run, largely because most of them have already been disposed of at the threshold of controversy.

Fundamentally, there are only two ways of dealing with a problem. Either you fight or you agree. Fighting, of course, may not take the form of war. It may take the form, let us say, of resisting a desegregation act. But this choice is always in one direction or the other. Ultimately, if those who are in power insist that their view must be carried out, and there is resistance, there must be resort to force. So that the only alternative to force, in the ultimate analysis, is compromise.

Another thing said by Lord Morley which is worth repeating, is that for disciples of the relative—and I take it most Americans are disciples of the relative—compromise was easy; but for the disciples of the absolute, compromise was impossible. A confusion sometimes assails the disciples of the relative when they are watching the activities of the disciples of the absolute. A man may have a passionate and absolute faith; but that does not mean he must insist that everybody else have it. So when Morley speaks of the absolute, he obviously has in mind attempts to enforce private beliefs in the forms of public life. Our Constitution wisely distinguishes between the two.

I should like to speak for a moment of our attitude to compromise today, at this very hour. We are going through—and I, for one, think we are by no means through with it—a long period of intolerance and obscurantism. As always happens in such periods, there is resort more and more in public opinion to absolute positions which tend to harden men's beliefs, and to make any form of compromise difficult. That resort to the absolute is evidenced today not only by the kind of intolerance with which we are all so familiar, but also by a return to that vague and fuzzy thing, fuzzy from the point of view, at least, of a Philadelphia lawyer—natural law. If natural law means those principles which describe a given faith, and if those who share that faith wish to use the prosaic word "law," I cannot greatly object. But if it means something that has always existed among decent people and should therefore be continued, I must differ. References of that kind merely obscure the problems we face.

The disciples of the absolute assert that we should never compromise with our enemies. Briand, that great statesman, had once been savagely attacked in the French Chambre des Deputés for saying that more assistance should be given to the new and rather weak German democracy under Stresemann. In answering, he said: "With whom should we try to get along except with our enemies?" It seems to me that very simple principle has been almost forgotten today.

Doesn't it miss the very essential meaning of diplomacy, which is give and take, and of having an ambassador at your enemy's court, when the Secretary of State—and it has happened to more than one Secretary of State on either side of the line—before going to Berlin announces that he will not compromise on a single issue? If you go to a conference to negotiate differences, and begin by announcing that you will make no compromises, you will not get very far. When you arrive in Berlin, you find that the mind of your opponent is closed, so that the words which follow are not even understood. In that connection is it not true that our modern technique of holding international conferences almost requires such a statement before a meeting? If international negotiations are held like political conventions—televised, broadcast, the reporters crowding around—it is inevitable that each statesman, trying to accomplish something deft, subtle, difficult, and enormously important, should be diverted from his purpose to talk defensively to that unknown, yet terrible, audience on the other side of the sea, watching every step that he makes and listening to every word that he says.

Compromise—largely through Munich—has come to mean appeasement. Munich distorted a wise and useful word. Cannot we get rid of that association of ideas, so that the tool of compromise can again be used when it is needed? Now more than ever *compromise* to the man in the street rings with something hidden and secret and conspiratorial. In reality, it is the principle on which our country was built.

Discussion at The Institute for Religious and Social Studies
January 17, 1956

Question: I should like to ask, sir, if you think there is a quite important and, perhaps for the diplomat, an essential difference between a compromise of a basic, moral principle to which he is committed, perhaps, and the kind of compromise that is necessary in working out political and diplomatic relations with your enemy? Maybe that is a purely academic distinction. I tried to put myself in the position of the Secretary of State and it seemed I would be forced to make those compromises all the time of the latter order but not of the former order.

Mr. Biddle: It may be that the fact that there are so few divines now engaged in political activity answers your question. But the question—if you will excuse my saying so—involves an ambiguity. The ambiguity is, do you mean compromise with yourself or compromise with the other fellow? You may not call his principles moral, but they are for him; and *vice versa*. I think it is a false division to put morals over here and politics over there. Principles are involved in political issues. Let me give you one, segregation today. Segregation is undoubtedly a moral principle for those who wish to abolish it, and it is also a principle among many Southerners who do not wish it abolished. Certainly history will sustain me when I suggest that the opposition to Abolition, through the ten years before the Civil War, was based on the Bible.

I do not think it fair to put on one side political issues and say morals do not belong in that field; and to put on the other side the great moral issues, suggesting that compromise is never appropriate in matters of moral conviction, though it may be in political issues.

I may be doing your question an injustice. I hope not.

Question: I wonder to what extent you relate the matter of compromise to the decision of the Supreme Court, in view of the dilemma which Virginia has posed and spread. How important is compromise in that area, and so forth?

Mr. Biddle: That is a very interesting question, one I have been thinking about a great deal. I am not sure I know the answer. The Supreme Court has in these decisions exercised a certain amount of compromise in the matter of timing, chiefly, in allowing a particular unit or locality to work out desegregation in its own way. In other words, it has compromised in those steps leading toward the eventual freeing of the schools. I suspect it will for a time continue to do that.

Question: Perhaps you could clarify why Munich which was a compromise, or which we always thought was a compromise, was wrong, and how we could have handled the situation?

Mr. Biddle: That is a mean question. I suppose that my rather broad sweep has opened me to it. Those who knew the state of the German armed machine at the time that compromise was made must have known that a show of strength could stop the German onslaught then. Munich was the conclusion of a series of stupid compromises, in my view. The first was over the crossing of the Rhine. The German army was exceedingly weak at the time, and France alone could have stopped it. Munich was the final act in that series.

The ultimate question is one of judgment. If you believe that this barbaric movement, tied to modern, scientific methods, superbly organized, and ready to spring, could have been prevented by fighting anywhere along the line, the answer depends on whether you believe in fighting at certain times. I do. One cannot argue about that. You either do or you don't. Another, subtler question is involved, which I, not being a Toynbee, am unable to answer. That is whether—like those measures which you suggested to me a little while ago were being taken in the Fourth Century in the Roman Empire and which did not prevent the ultimate debacle —the measures we might have taken before Munich and might be taking now, will stop the deluge or not: That I am unprepared to say.

Question: Do you feel there might have been any form of compromise either in timing or otherwise that could have prevented the Civil War and still preserved the Union?

Mr. Biddle: I feel I have graduated from being a Philadelphia lawyer to being an historian with a vision. I think at the proper time compromise would have been possible. Most of the great Southerners were opposed to slavery. The South did not realize that her soil was almost gone. They couldn't go on with the cotton plantations, and slave labor was no longer economically valuable. If anything could have been done to delay the decision over a few more years, the new era of the industrialist was coming so fast that I think slavery could have been stopped; but how, or when, I couldn't tell you.

Question: Did I understand you to say now that you come to a point where you agree to fight or don't agree to fight and that would be a point of no compromise in your point of view? I want to ask this question: in view of the fact that the world now has the means of self-annihilation, would that knowledge cause you to place this absolute, you would or wouldn't fight, would that cause you to change your mind at that point?

Mr. Biddle: I cannot imagine a situation in which I would use the bomb. Is that the simplest way of putting it?

Question: Not quite.

Mr. Biddle: All I mean is you must always determine whether you want to get your way enough to fight. It is perfectly true war today is more than fighting; it may be annihilation. So that choice takes on an entirely new aspect. But the choice exists, does it not? Either you have to let go on what you don't want and let the other fellow have his way or fight. The alternative is the same.

II

THE LOYALTY OF THE PRIEST

JOHN LAFARGE, S.J.

I have been asked to discuss the question of dilemmas, in relation to the life of a priest. A clergyman's life, after all, is rarely without its dilemmas and each dilemma leads to another.

The other day I noticed an old-fashioned woodcut on the masthead of a highbrow paper published on the West Coast. A highly symbolic picture represented a walrus floating in the Pacific Ocean. A bear was seated on the walrus. It pictured a perfect dilemma. If the bear continued sitting on the walrus he would starve to death, and if he ate the walrus he would drown. But at least the bear was conscious of his plight.

Sometimes people do not know that they are in some of the worst dilemmas. Take the hypothetical case of a United States Senator who might be chairman of a subcommittee investigating subversion and, at the same time, organizes a campaign to nullify the Constitution of the United States. He does not realize the contradiction, but the contradiction exists.

One source of our dilemmas is the question of conflicting loyalties and identifications.

The other day a friend wrote me, a young priest who is doing active work in the State of South Carolina. He is obliged to travel forty miles each way, once a week, in order to obtain milk for the children of his congregation. Since his congregation is not of the Caucasian race, he cannot obtain any milk or other supplies in the town where he dwells.

The source of the difficulty is, of course, that he has identified himself with the people for whom he is working. He is known as

9

"one of them." He experiences the problem of a man who becomes identified with his people in a way that would cause embarrassment. A familiar term is used to express such affiliation, let us say, with the Negro group—a word used in certain parts of the country which I will not repeat, implying that a person has a particular affection or interest in that group: a term of opprobrium.

We can of course take a clearcut heroic attitude and banish further consideration. Nevertheless, the question deserves a little exploring. A person is identified by his activities, interests or education; or he may be identified passively because he accepts the lot of the people for whom he works. This may be a racial group or some other group, but one much affected by social differences. In this country, as I see it, the main social differences are between racial and cultural groups rather than between the economic classes. In the European countries the abyss to be crossed is the harsh separation between the rich and the poor. Here it is more apt to result from differences in status or in race—something which is hard to explain to people of other lands.

The Gospels tell us, of course, that we should glory in such identification with the poor and the humiliated. Yet objections occur. The clergyman in this situation finds himself accused of being disloyal to his *own* group or race. In many suburban communities he is accused of being disloyal to the neighborhood, because he is not contributing to the preservation of its integrity—a neighborhood which has been built up with great effort over a number of years, by people proud of its traditions. Through his concern with another group, he is upsetting that neighborhood's integrity.

A further embarrassment can trouble him. Certain subversive elements in the community, such as Communists, use his voluntary identification as a means for their own propaganda. Consequently, he falls under suspicion. A difficulty may come from the group itself. For instance, they realize the man who is "in charge" of them, the clergyman who has devoted his life to their own welfare, is no longer a man of standing in the general community; that he is regarded with suspicion, and they may have lost a champion.

Then somebody else says, very persuasively: "Why identify your-self anyhow with one group of people? Be friends to all people." Why not be identified with the lot of any and all groups? In singling one group out, aren't we destroying many fine, old traditions? For us here in the North it is hard to realize the strength of the South's feeling about the old traditions, and about the person who is dis-loyal to them.

So, to make the dilemma precise, it comes to a question of divided loyalty: loyalty to the people of your choice, as well as to the people of your natural origin and of your environment—loyalty to the State in which you live; loyalty to your country, in the case of the agitation of subversives.

Added to this is the question of one's own limits. The moment you adopt an identification with any type of people for whom you labor, you set a limit on yourself. It is somewhat the situation that confronts a devoted schoolmaster. The headmaster is a marked man. Through his very absorption in the mind of the young, he develops a schoolmaster's mind. He becomes a wonderful Mr. Chips whom his own pupils remember with great fondness. But then he has cut himself off, in a way, from the rest of the world.

The difficulty is heightened by the mistakes and excesses of those whom he befriends. People complain: we, too, are little men; we, too, are sufferers; our rights, too, are being injured. I need not de-velop that theme. Instances are numerous.

A book which has recently appeared, by James Baldwin, a Negro writer, entitled *Notes of a Native Son* (Beacon Press), illustrates some of the oddities experienced by those who are racially identified by birth, not by choice. Mr. Baldwin is perhaps unduly sensitive. Nevertheless, one forgives his sensitivity in view of the acuteness of his perception. A chapter describes his experience in visiting Switzer-land and living in a Swiss village. In many ways it was delightful. He was with people who had none of our traditional race prejudice. He was simply a physical curiosity, an oddity: so much so that the children would want to touch his skin and hair with their fingers. He was not identified with the tradition of the slave, as in this country; he was not associated with one side of a long and angry dispute, nor with the troubles and trials and excitement of a minority group's long period of evolution. He was classified with the world's curiosities—with people who have six toes or are eight feet high. It was a strange experience, and hard to assimilate. So he shrewdly draws a conclusion. After all, when he came back home, in spite of the many things that grieved his heart, he became a *real* person. Even if others misunderstood him or had bitter feelings against him, nevertheless he was real. He would rather be misunderstood as a real person than be an unreal individual treated as an object but not as a human being.

Then, of course, you see the other side of the picture—a certain snobbery of philanthropy, a snobbery of the liberal type—not the genuine liberal, but what Russell Kirk refers to as the "ritualistic liberal," the type that feels he must be a liberal on every possible occasion, without regard for anything else. That is also a problem.

So, without wearying you further, I ask how we may resolve this difficulty. If the motive of voluntary identification, such as I described in the case of my friend in South Carolina, is mere sentiment, mere human sentimentality, we do not escape the dilemma. Your sentiments are met by other people's sentiments, and their sentiments are met by further reaction on your part, and you revolve in a vicious circle. But as a priest, I look in another direction. I naturally turn to the Scriptures, the history of God's dealing with man, and I notice a very wonderful thing which is the cornerstone of my religious belief, a profound element which is the mysterious fact—I say "mysterious" in the truest sense of the word—that the Creator does identify Himself with the creature. From the very first beginning of Genesis the Scripture story reveals how God has made Himself one with the human race. God is not just sitting up there as a majestic being to be approached with reverence and humility, fear and trembling, but He is living and working and suffering and thinking with men, as it were. He has compassion, not on abstractions, but on *us,* as persons. The biblical point of view—in the Old Testament, or the New Testament of Jesus, our

Lord—is a deep sense of solicitude, not for an abstract evil that is *in* men, but for the men who are suffering evil. Our Judeo-Christian point of view seems to differ from the Oriental philosophies in that we are interested not so much in combating the evil as something which somehow exists in people, as we are interested in them, themselves. It is a direct approach to the human personality, to the dignity of the human person.

So, for that reason, I think the question of identifying ourselves with a certain group ultimately comes to our attitude toward them as persons—the personal point of view. Again, I accept the limitation. Certain boundaries are inherent in the reality of our approach to life. Any real approach to human relations, to any work in which we try to bring God into people's lives, implies a certain boundary to what we can do. We cannot be all things. We cannot be a universal identification which is a universal nonidentification. To be real, we must, like Mr. Chips, recognize certain limits and suffer the consequences thereof.

Finally, the heart of any genuine dealing with this whole question is the realization of common interests. Our identification with the interests of a certain group, a certain class of people, means to work *with them* for the interests of all. One of the cardinal points of my friend in the South is to bring home to his own people—the people he is working for and to his "own people" in the other sense, the people of his natural origin—that their interests are one, that he is not working for the black man or working for the white man, but that they are working with him for the common good.

In this matter of race relations the real battlefront is right in our own communities, in our own neighborhoods all over the country, in fact, all over the expanding world. Everywhere the real question becomes one of people realizing the common interests of all.

That is sometimes difficult for people to grasp, but all of us can contribute. I am hopeful that in the end I am not reduced to the painful situation of the bear seated on the walrus, nor to the dilemma of the truculent Senator and his conflicting policies. I think there are ways out even of these most difficult dilemmas.

Discussion at The Institute for Religious and Social Studies
January 10, 1956

Question: Many of us have to live with the "ritualistic liberal"
you described and many of us often find ourselves tempted to behave as "ritualistic liberals." Don't you think there is a bit of hope
for the "ritualistic liberal," that he can grow, perhaps by hearing you?

Father LaFarge, S.J.: In point of fact, it comes down to this. We regard certain things in our society as needing reform or not, and it depends on whether we are serious about the reform. There is a great
deal of humbug and confusion in the matter of social reform, of
course. Nevertheless, no real reform I know has ever been accomplished without intense application and a certain amount of par-
tisanship. In other words, if something is really to be done, say a
law is to be passed, if things are to be accomplished, it does need a
certain partiality and devotion. When I speak of the "ritualistic
liberal," I am using the term merely in quotes. The "ritualistic
liberal" would be the individual who would be liberal from mere
compulsion, feeling he must take a liberal attitude on everything
just for the sake of being liberal. On the other hand, a concrete liberal
position is necessary if we are going to accomplish anything. It is
necessary for people to become identified with a cause, more or less
to lose themselves in it, to do a certain amount of foolishness, perhaps, a certain amount of imprudence. I remember some years ago
one of my own colleagues in a Western university making a fool
of himself. This university was closed to people of other races. He
made a fool of himself by doing a foolish thing. He made an address
which everybody said was imprudent. So much so, he was removed for
reason of his indiscretion. Yet two years later what he had asked
for took place. Objectively, what he did was imprudent, but prac-
tically, not. When I look back on my own life, I find I did a lot
of things I shouldn't have done and I wouldn't do over again in
the same position, and yet, I am now very thankful I did them.

Question: Father LaFarge, in regard to the hypothetical Senator
to whom you referred, is that a recurrent problem with which we
are constantly faced, or do you consider that part of a passing

phenomenon which is now no longer an acute problem as it once was?

Father LaFarge, S.J.: I pray it is passing, but it is acute at the present moment. As I said, the gentleman in this state of dilemma would not recognize it as a dilemma.

Question: Would you expand your theme? What is the right relationship between sacred zeal and patience?

Father LaFarge, S.J.: A sacred zeal as I understand it, according to the definitions of the Fathers of the Church, is a love, a real, genuine, fervent, I would say *bona fide* love for spreading the truth. In other words, if I really believe in the existence of God and I am living among people who do not believe in God, I have a sacred zeal for spreading and diffusing the belief in God, because I feel I owe it to God and I owe it to my fellow men. Now, if it is a sacred zeal, my motive is lofty and pure. It would not be a sacred zeal if in so doing I allow in myself the element of dogmatism, of impatience, of disrespect for human personality, and so on. In other words, what would be my attitude? My attitude toward the people who do not believe in God is to present them with the reasons why I think they should believe in God. I present them with the arguments that appeal to me, for better or worse, and I speak to them frankly and say, "Brother, I think you are mistaken," and I tell them the consequences of the mistake and give them my reasons. But I would not try to force their minds. You cannot force another person's mind.

That I would consider a sacred zeal. I would consider it an unsacred zeal if I hit a man over the head and said, "Believe in God, or else!" Patience is a part of it. I have to be patient. I can have sacred zeal and patience both. In fact the idea of patience is part of its sacredness, God has zeal for us. He wants us to fulfil His commandments, and His zeal for us is infinite; yet He is extraordinarily patient.

Question: When you said there was a dilemma in going against one's own tradition in the society in which one is reared, I thought, after all there is the question of right and wrong and the Will of God; there is no dilemma, especially if you are a clergyman, even if you are not a clergyman. But I thought further, there is an eternal dilemma—this eternal dilemma between the world in which we are raised and the world we want. We have an allegiance to the tradition we are raised in simply because it brought us up, we got to be adult by living there. So this kind of loyalty to traditions in the South is really a dilemma. That is how they are brought up, and they have to go against their fathers, so to speak, and it becomes a family dilemma—disrespect for the word of the parent. That is an eternal dilemma which faces us in the problem of war.

Can you comment on how we face these problems?

Father LaFarge, S.J.: What you say is acute and true. You brought it out better than I did, possibly, with regard to the situation in Southern communities. Those who have lived under those circumstances know how painful it can be. When you are faced with such an alternative you feel shock and pain. You are doing something upsetting to sacred and hallowed traditions. There again, the biblical point of view is one of respect for the traditions.

You suddenly jump to the question of war. There, of course, I don't know whether your question is about the dilemma between war and pacifism. That presents a tremendous question. You wanted my view on that?

Question: World pacifism, from a religious point of view, creates a dilemma of loyalty to one's country as well as loyalty to the tradition we are raised in.

Father LaFarge, S.J.: Let me put it this way. We can have loyalty to our country and loyalty to the world community and those two views are not exclusive. Just as in this country we are loyal to our State, to our local community, and also to our national community. I am loyal to my Church and to my country. I not only see no contradiction but I think the two loyalties are complementary.

I think we have to impress a very fundamental thing difficult for many to suppose. Nevertheless, there is a loyalty to the world community.

Let us put a concrete example. On the front page of *The New York Times* today [January 10, 1956] there is the question of farm surplus. Certainly the question of farm surplus cannot be solved merely on the question of loyalty to our own country. It is outrageous to argue about it merely from the point of view of the interests of our own nation. It has to be seen in relation to the world community. We will never have a solution to the question of our farm surplus until we see it in relation to the needs of the hundreds of millions of starving people all over the world. There is no solution in my mind, to the farm problem on a purely national basis. The farm problem today is an international problem. It is when we begin to see these things as international problems that we approach more closely to a solution of the agonizing dilemma of war and peace.

We are talking particularly about loyalty. Many people have the idea that you can have only one loyalty. We can have a hierarchy of loyalties, and the lower loyalty is affected by the higher loyalty. I am a loyal citizen of the City of New York. I don't do anything against its regulations. I don't park my car on the wrong side of the street: I wouldn't even if I had a car. But I am also loyal to my country. I am loyal to my Church. I am loyal to the world community. The dilemma there is simply the question of means. The terrible situation in the world today concerns the most available means to preserve peace. I cannot say that pacifism is a solution. I wish it were. But that brings us down to the dilemmas of the ultimate situation about the hydrogen bomb, and I was trying to steer away from that because it is pretty much beyond me.

III

COMPROMISE AND POLITICS

BY

EUGENE J. McCARTHY

Politics has been defined as the art of the possible. It is not a science which determines the elements of the good life, but one which depends upon the findings of other disciplines. Strictly speaking, it is not an ethical science; yet it is, of course, related to ethics and is dependent upon ethics for its goals and for the determination of its standards of procedure. The objective of politics is to bring about progressive change in keeping with the demands of social justice. Politics is concerned with ways and means and with prudential determinations as to what should be done, when it should be done, in what measure it should be done, and how it should be done. In working out the answers to these questions, compromise is called for.

Politicians are expected to be compromised, to compromise, yet they are ordinarily criticized for being compromisers. The writings of Machiavelli, together with all of the associations that go with his name, have placed a burden upon politics and upon politicians, and have given a bad name and significance to compromise. As a matter of fact, of course, politicians are not the only compromisers in human society. Compromise is the mark of human relations, not only in politics, but in almost every institution or social relationship involving two or more persons. Genuine compromise is not a violation of principle, not a compromise with principle, but with reality.

This common attitude toward politics and toward compromise is reflected in a letter which I received recently from a professor of economics, advising me as to what my position should be on a certain piece of legislation being considered by the Congress. He concluded his letter by saying that he assumed he was wasting his time since I would probably not do what was indicated by sound economics, but would act on the basis of politics. I wrote back saying that I did not believe in the primacy of economics and that I did not think that political decisions and economic decisions could be placed and judged in the relationship of one to the other in the same order. Economics is, the economists say, a science, and, of course, politicians have a responsibility to give attention to the knowledge which this science has developed; but in the political decision which was called for, there were many things other than economic considerations involved. I might have quoted Edmund Burke's observation that the number of factors bearing upon any particular political decision is infinite, and consequently the number of solutions which may be proposed is also infinite. I do not think that this would have satisfied him any more than the answer which I did give. It must be remembered, however, that political decisions cannot be based purely upon the determinations of science or of philosophy, but must take into account the whole history of mankind, together with the particular conditions existing at the time of decision.

Politics is a part of the real world. In politics the simple choice between that which is wholly right and that which is wholly wrong is seldom given; the ideal is not often realized, and in some cases cannot even be advocated. Political leaders, in what Maritain describes as a "regressive or barbarous society," may have their freedom of choice reduced to the point where they must take a position which is questionable, rather than the alternative which is simply and wholly bad. The choice involved is not one of the lesser of two evils, really, but the choice of that which has some good in it, no matter how limited. Prudence may require the toleration of a measure of evil in order to prevent something worse, or to save the limited good. The principle of double effect is here involved. It is the good effect, limited though it be, which is willed and desired, not the evil which must be tolerated. Prudence may dictate a decision to let the cockle grow with the wheat.

It seems that as long as man lives with his conscience there is an area in which he can exercise free choice. Even, if we can tell from reports, in the nightmare of society, in the concentrational political order of Buchenwald, an area of free and responsible choice remained.

The fact that politics involves compromise and difficult choices does not give us an excuse for neglecting it. As Henry Lefevre has written: "One can be pure or responsible in politics; he cannot be both." And Thomas More, writing in *Utopia,* expressed the same idea in these words: "If evil opinion and naughty persuasion cannot be utterly and altogether plucked out of their hearts; if you cannot, even as you would, remedy vices which habit and custom have confirmed, yet this is no cause for leaving and forsaking the commonwealth."

Many people are hesitant to enter politics because they feel that they will have to make compromises. Of course they will. Even the preliminary choice of party involves some compromise. There are few, if any, people, I am quite sure, who would say that either the program of the Democratic party or that of the Republican party is entirely acceptable to them. There is, of course, greater freedom in our party system than there is in the British system, where party discipline is enforced with greater vigor. The only really pure position offered on a national ticket in the United States is that of the Vegetarians. It may be that what is here involved is not really a question of principle, but in any case it is a pure position and does offer one a rather narrow but an absolute and clearly defined position and program.

One of the best statements on the whole question of compromise is contained in the essay on "Compromise" by Lord Morley. In this essay he states that the interesting and basic question really involved in compromise is not one of principle against principle, but one that turns upon the placing of the boundary that divides wise suspense in forming opinions, wise reserve in expressing them, and wise tardiness in trying to realize them, from unavowed disingenuousness, from self-delusion, from voluntary dissemination, ignorance, and pusillanimity.

Oftentimes in passing judgment upon politicians in the United

States, we do not allow for compromise. It is common, particularly in campaigns, that the incumbents are attacked as compromisers, and for the challengers to insist that their approach to politics and to the problem of government will be a moral one, or in some cases, a spiritual one; but that in any case, it will not be political. Of course, once established in office, those whose approach was that of the purist are ordinarily called upon to make concessions to realities and to become in some measure compromisers and thereby practitioners of the art of politics.

Actually the compromises which a member of the United States Congress is called upon to make fall into perhaps four general categories. There is the compromise which is one of degree, a quantitative one which arises when we have a choice of getting nothing, or getting something short of what we want. This kind of compromise is called for, or at least must be considered, on almost every controversial issue which comes before the Congress.

On the Immigration Act, for example, the choice was not whether we would have a perfect bill, or whether we would accept something short of perfection; but the final choice was between taking a bill which had some good things in it and some bad things in it, or a bill which had some other bad things in it, and some other good things in it. No matter what choice was made, it involved a compromise. It involved accepting something which fell short of the ideal.

The same problem arises regularly, for example, on tax legislation, which is complicated and involved. I suppose that no member is ever entirely satisfied with the final draft accepted by Congress. And the same is true, in large measure, of appropriations bills. Compromises of this kind are generally not too difficult to defend. We can make a case for concession because in exchange for concession some measure of good is accomplished. The provision in the House rules for a motion to recommit, seldom sends a bill back to the committee. What it does, generally, is to allow the members to record a qualification in their support for the bill, and having made that record a member may feel free to vote for the bill on final passage. It is the closest thing to a "maybe" or qualified vote provided for the Congress.

A second kind of compromise that may be called for is more in the nature of a qualitative one, involving principle in some measure. It arises when we are faced with the difficult choice of giving up a genuine issue in exchange for action on some other important issue. Compromise of this kind arises, for example, in connection with amendments dealing with the problem of racial discrimination and segregation. In recent Congresses, segregation amendments have been proposed in connection with at least three important bills —one on housing, another on Federal aid to education, and a third on military manpower. In each case the argument was made that if the amendment was adopted the program itself would fail. The problem of the member of Congress was to decide whether he would go on record for the segregation question; a matter of principle—with the possiblity that if the amendment passed, the housing legislation would be defeated, or that the education bill would fail to pass, or that the military manpower program would be rejected.

In each case the problem is slightly different. Since everyone's home, in a sense, is segregated from everyone else's home, families do not suffer from segregation in this respect as they do as individuals in public institutions such as schools. The segregation amendment to the education bill should be weighed in the light of the Supreme Court decision and its recommendation of gradual change. In passing judgment on the question of a segregation amendment to an armed services manpower bill, the whole matter of national defense, of course, if this were of vital consideration, would have to be weighed. And on the other hand, the experience of the past war and of the postwar period, in which military desegregation orders have been in effect and have worked out quite well, has to be taken into account. The practical problem involves the prudential determination as to what should be done in each of the three cases.

The third area of compromise, or at least an area in which we must face the question of compromise, is that of means and methods. Assuming that our purposes are good and that we are agreed on principle, there arises the question as to how we can best accomplish the goals which we have set. We all agree that applying intrinsically evil means to attain intrinsically good ends cannot be justified. The means we use must be proportionate to the ends which we are seeking. In a democratic society we must be particularly concerned about the question of means, since we must be right not only about our goals and purposes, but also right with regard to the method and the devices by which we seek to accomplish those goals. We must be particularly alert when all too often the question of success is the only standard to be applied. We cannot use the same devices as our enemies and proceed, as one man in high government position urged a year or two ago, as fanatics approaching the problem of international relations with "no holds barred." We must remember that if we compromise on the means, in a sense we have already admitted our own defeat.

Under ordinary circumstances we must tell the truth. Of course, in time of war we do not have to expose to the enemy our every plan. Our rule must be that of whether or not the individual, the nation, or the institution which is asking or seeking information has a right to that information. Difficult problems arise in these in-between times—times of neither war nor peace. For example, the question must be raised as to how much information the citizens of a democracy have a right to on government policies in international problems. I suppose we could settle the question in principle by saying that citizens have a right to whatever information is necessary to their making the political decisions which they are called upon to make. If, of course, granting such information might have the effect of prejudicing our position in international affairs, a government might justify some kind of restraint, some kind of withholding. In general, however, the citizen has the right to whatever information is necessary for him to make the basic decisions which he is called upon to make.

We have, then, an additional question of what kind of information we can give to other peoples throughout the world. Certainly in this respect I do not think that the times justify our proceeding as "fanatics" and "with no holds barred." The peoples who are looking to our leadership or who are considering accepting our leadership (or at least going along with us) in international affairs, have a right to whatever information is necessary for them to make their decisions. We do not have an obligation to publish all of our national sins or to show our worst side to the peoples of the world, but, on the other hand, we do have an obligation to give them a truthful picture of what kind of people we are and what we really believe.

Very recently with some Congressional urging, the United States Information Service withdrew a book from circulation in our libraries abroad. Among the charges made against this book was one that it contained an essay by Thoreau advocating civil disobedience. It was an anthology of American writing. If, of course, the only thing in the book had been an essay advocating civil disobedience, I think we would agree that it was not representative of American thought. But it contained, in addition to this essay, selections from almost every American writer of any note. In addition to written selections it also contained pictures. There was great protest against one of the pictures—that of a schoolroom in New England. The basis of the protest, so far as I have been able to discover, was that the school teacher was not pretty. She was from Vermont and looked as Vermonters are reputed to look. Moreover, one of her students had a patch on the seat of his pants. It was argued that this kind of picture did not truly represent American education, and that Russian propaganda pieces showed very pretty school teachers. It should have been argued that we have different criteria than have the Russians.

A fourth general area in which the problem of compromise arises is that of the whole matter of representation in Congress. Assuming that he could determine their position, is a member of Congress to accept that his function is simply to represent the position of the majority of his people? If this were the case, I suppose with the techniques of the Gallup Poll, or similar polling techniques more widely established, a member could ask for a poll of his district on any issue, or on a number of issues, and then record his vote as indicated in the poll. There are a few members of Congress who conduct private polls. Most of them, however, protest that they do not base their decisions on the result of the poll, but rather use it as an indication of what the people in the district are thinking and then proceed to vote according to their own good judgment and to persuade the people of their error if the Congressman's action differs from the position of the people as indicated in the poll.

On this question of representative government, I suppose that if we are satisfied that the people of our district are informed adequately on an issue and that the position is fixed in their minds, we might make a case for acting in keeping with the majority position. On this basis we can make an excuse for Southern members of Congress taking the stand that they do on the race question. Since it is generally accepted that it would be political suicide for anyone from the South boldly to oppose what appears to be the prevailing Southern attitude on the question, it is accepted that for a Southern member of Congress to take a firm stand on this question would lead to his inevitable defeat. And it is argued that his replacement would probably be wrong not only on this issue, but on many other issues. Supposedly, a member involved in this situation might quietly vote the belief of the majority of his people. He would not, however, be justified in making speeches and declaring that his belief coincided with that of the majority of his people, if this were not true. As times change and a member becomes uncertain as to how the people of his district may stand on an issue, he would certainly have some obligation occasionally to make a test of the change and to take a stand which, in his opinion, was the right one to take. He has an obligation to run some risk, to be slightly ahead of what may be a backward position on the part of the people of his district. He must hope that by his action and by his influence, and even in some cases possibly by his political death, he may advance the cause of justice.

In another case, however, a member who is from a district in which people are indifferent on an issue of this kind would have a clear obligation not to compromise, but to take a firm and clear stand. Concerning new issues about which people are not and cannot be well informed, it is my opinion that the member of Congress has the responsibility to inform himself, and then, according to his best judgment, proceed to act in the hope that he can defend his action to the people of his district. Edmund Burke faced this problem and analyzed it, I think rather well, in his essay on the responsibility of a representative in a democracy. Burke was in difficulty in the course of his campaign on three issues: foreign policy, finance, and religion. He appealed to the electorate to have confidence in the judgment of their representatives and to permit them to act upon a varied and a large view of things. If this is not granted, he said, at length the national representation would be infallibly degraded into a confused and scuttling bustle of local agency. When the popular member—the representative, that is— he said, is narrowed and rendered timid in his proceedings, the service of the crown will be the sole nursery of statesmen. Then the monopoly of mental power will be added to all other powers that he possesses. On the side of the people there will be nothing but impotence, for ignorance is impotence; narrowness of mind is impotence; timidity is itself ignorance and makes all other qualities that go along with it impotent and useless.

Burke was, as I recall, defeated in the election following this defense of himself, but he did come back successfully in a later election and went on to serve admirably in the British Parliament.

There are problems of compromise, also, in the field of foreign affairs which in their very nature are perhaps no different from the compromises called for in the field of domestic legislation. As we do make compromises along the way in foreign relations, as we do accept partial victories or even give ground in the hope of greater success some time later, we must keep in mind that there are broad and basic principles which should govern our international affairs, just as there are broad and basic principles which should govern, or at least be weighed and considered, in making decisions in the area of domestic problems. In the field of foreign affairs there are at least three broad moral issues that we need to keep in mind. One is that of the poverty of other people throughout the world. The second is that of the cultural differences between us and other people and our responsibility to bring them truth. And the third is that of racial antagonism and racial prejudice. Each decision and compromise along the way should be judged in view of its contribution or its bearing upon the solution of these great overriding problems.

The politician and the moralist have a great deal in common. Moralists, said Maritain, are unhappy people—so are politicians. "When the moralists insist on the immutability of moral principles," continued Maritain, "they are reproached for imposing unlivable requirements on us. When they explain the way in which these immutable principles are to be put into force, taking into account the diversity of concrete situations, they are reproached for making morality relative. In both cases, however, they are only upholding the claims of reason to direct life. The task of ethics," said Maritain, "is a humble one but it is also magnanimous in carrying the mutable application of immutable moral principles even in the midst of the agonies of an unhappy world as far as there is in it a gleam of humanity."

The task of the politician is, in a sense, even more humble than that of the moralist. Ours is not the responsibility of making the decision, but rather a more menial responsibility of putting it into effect. The politician, of course, must be a moralist himself, and he must harken to the voice of the moralist. As he proceeds in action, his general guide must be to make his decisions in the hope that by these decisions an imperfect world may become somewhat more perfect, or that, at least, if he cannot make an imperfect world somewhat less imperfect, he can save it from becoming even less perfect or finally from becoming entirely evil and perverted. He can try to prevent degradation; to prevent decline; and, if possible, to move things forward and upward toward right and justice. That is the purpose and the end of political action and of the compromises that go with that action.

IV

THE SOCIAL RESPONSIBILITY OF THE SCIENTIST

BY

I. I. RABI

I have had no training in the consideration of life's dilemmas. However, when I was asked to speak on this subject, it was a long time ago, and it did seem as if life were full of problems and dilemmas, and that I would have no difficulty. It was very different when I began to think about it particularly.

Some people go through life as if they were traversing a labyrinth or maze, where every turn presents a new problem which somehow must be solved by an appeal to first principles. These are the problem seekers and problem solvers—the moralists, the people who feel that there is always a specific right or wrong to every course of action. They are the salt of the earth, although often the trial and worry of their friends. Without them we would not have our great ethical systems. With them we have problems which led to Socrates drinking the hemlock.

Others, of which I happen to be one, tend to see life in the broad perspective. They fix their aims on a distant goal without any great hope of reaching it. But they try, in so far as possible, to tend in that general direction. Knowing that the road is long, they tend to take the easier path so as not to tire themselves for the journey. To such people, life does not present itself as a series of problems but, rather, as a landscape within which there are hills and rivers, paths and shortcuts which form a certain pattern. The approach is empirical and compromising, but the general movement is in the forward direction toward a goal.

I had not thought about this matter very seriously until I was confronted with the necessity of giving this paper on "Life's Problems and Dilemmas." This paper, in fact, constitutes my first serious problem. Before this, I could always see them coming and take proper evasive action. My own point of view is, I feel, natural for a pure scientist. An engineer or scientist who works on practical problems is under the obligation to try to solve them whether they are interesting to him or not, whether they are difficult or easy. His life is full of problems which he must meet head on. The pure scientist, however, has as his choice the whole of the unknown, and he can pick and choose those fields of endeavor which are congenial to his nature and to his abilities.

This attitude is sanctioned by society and tradition. To do anything else would defeat the whole meaning of pure uncommitted research. The great discoveries in science have rarely been made through a projection of the known but, rather, as a result of the observation of seemingly irrelevant phenomena. In this way Becquerel discovered radioactivity, because he happened to leave some plates in his desk drawer close to some keys, there was some pitchblende nearby, and in developing the plates he noticed something odd. Heinrich Hertz while engaged in his research on the electromagnetic nature of light noticed an obscure little phenomenon where sparks came out in certain circumstances and did not in others. He took the side path and discovered the phenomenon of photoelectricity which is the basis of the photoelectric cell.

I do not suggest that everyone who devotes himself to pure science has the same attitude. Some tend to look upon the problems of research as a series of challenges which they must meet or feel cowardly and inadequate. Such people evoke great admiration. Their accomplishments and honors are truly deserved. But they sometimes miss a great deal of the inner meaning of scientific endeavor.

When I consider some of the important decisions I have had to make in my time, they seem hardly to have involved any serious soulsearching, although I now realize that others could have made a thorough job of such an occasion.

Quite early in my teens I decided I wanted to be a scientist. I did not know any scientists but I had read a great deal of biography of scientists. Furthermore, the majestic range and profundity of science matched very closely the deep religious questions which were continually discussed in the Orthodox Jewish home in which I grew up. I had no idea of how one became a scientist or what the name was of the science which was closest to my real interest. It was not until I was twenty-four that I realized that the field of science in which I was really interested was called physics.

Somewhere along the road, I made up my mind that since I expected to live only once, if possible I would not work at anything which did not have an important significance to me. Therefore, after I had discovered physics, other interests, which were many, receded into the background. There was no necessity for conscious dedication because the extent and depth of the subject is enough to contain most of the horizon of anyone who has a taste for this kind of endeavor. An active physicist with an outside hobby is a rarity.

Thus, when I obtained a small fellowship from Columbia after receiving the Ph.D. degree, I accepted it for the purpose of continuing my studies in Europe. Even though jobs were scarce, this meant resigning the position at the College of the City of New York where I had obtained a small foothold and leaving my newly wed wife at home for a period of one to two years. Even though the prospects for obtaining another job on my return were bleak, no other decision was thinkable once the direction of my life was fixed.

The decade following my return saw the rise of Hitler, the bitter Spanish Civil War, and the economic depression. It also saw the rededication of the United States to the high ideals of the Founding Fathers. In the same period, the United States came to intellectual maturity in science. The decade 1929 to 1939 saw the United States assume the role of intellectual endeavor appropriate to its size and welfare. At the beginning of this decade we were provincial in science, limited in outlook, and unsure in our taste. At the end we led the whole world.

I was very happy with my part in this great awakening of science in this country. During these ten years I was hardly away from my laboratory for more than five days or nights in the year. Although the threatening prospects in Europe hung as a pall over our lives, in the laboratory all was joy and gaiety. We sang at our work and counted every hour away from it as a loss. All of our experiments were hard and trying, mentally and physically. The rewards and the new insights we gained were more than adequate compensation.

The fall of France in 1940 changed the whole prospect. Not only was our country threatened by the Nazi juggernaut, but all of civilization—all values, spiritual, moral, intellectual—were in danger of being betrayed, destroyed by the Nazi beasts. I felt this very strongly, not only as a citizen, as a scientist, but in a deep, personal way.

Therefore, it was not with regret but with joy that I closed my laboratory after the fall of France, more than a year before we entered the war officially, and went off to Cambridge, Massachusetts, together with some of my closest associates, to organize the radiation laboratory. Our job was to use our scientific talents to invent and develop new weapons to defeat the enemy of mankind.

None of us had ever had any modern military experience of any kind. For most of us our new tasks which were in the field of radar were quite unfamiliar. Very few had ever worked at any field of applied science. We had to remake our personalities and attitudes. We had to deal with military people and commercial organizations, rather than with deans and department chairmen.

Strangely enough, we found the transition to be an easy one. We were young and brash. Full of self-confidence, we did not really think that we had serious problems in meeting situations which were new and unfamiliar. We did not seek advice and, therefore, the cutting edge of our determination was not blunted by vague fears and misgivings. Instead of reforming ourselves, we took the easier road and reformed the military to our way of thinking and doing. There was no frivolity in this attitude. We were entirely conscious that the future of civilization was at stake and that the cumbersome traditional procedures would give us too little and too late.

After the initial shock of surprise, we were completely accepted by the military. They realized our aim was to help them and not to carve out careers for ourselves. The close relations which exist in this country between science and the military were made from the successful symbiosis of the war years. A military man is trained to command men, to be brave, resourceful, and to fight. In the technological rear, his weapons come from people who are at the frontier of scientific knowledge and who can foresee technology which is imminent in the newest discoveries of basic science. The tactics for the deployment of these weapons is, again, the task of the military.

This symbiosis between science and the military is perhaps the most important and newest social and political development of this century. Never before have so many scientists of high caliber and unlimited means devoted themselves to the problem of killing people and disrupting their whole social organization of production, distribution, transportation, and communication. Compared with the problems in basic science, killing people and disorganizing modern, complex human society is easy. We must face the fact that in the near future the destruction of all that we call civilization and decent living will be simple and economical. The means for accomplishing these ends will not be a matter of speculation but will actually exist, ready for instant action.

This autobiographical introduction is by way of approach to the problem which you really expected me to discuss—"The Social Responsibility of a Scientist." First of all I want to say I do not consider it to be a problem of the scientist alone. It is a problem for the statesman, for the teacher, for the man of religion, for the molders of public opinion—the press, radio, television—for everybody. This is life's problem and dilemma for our day and for all the future, as long as our technological civilization continues to exist.

The problem will become more difficult every day that passes without some concrete and sincere action taken to cope with it. The scientist has indeed a serious social responsibility for the application of his discovery, but he has no authority to decide in which direction his discovery will be applied. Responsibility without authority is a meaningless term in the realm of practical action. Of course, he can wash his hands of the whole affair and cease being a scientist. But suicide has never been considered to be a highly moral solution to ethical problems.

To my mind, the scientist discharges his special responsibility by informing his fellow citizens and the world of the consequences of the application of his discoveries. After that he has the responsibility of every other lawabiding citizen of equal intellectual and ethical endowment. When a collective decision is taken, he cannot, as member of one group, arrogantly stand apart from the rest of society on which he depends for support and sustenance. To expect anything else from as large and varied a group as the scientific community is chimerical.

Having discharged my social responsibility, I would like to join with you in wrestling with the dilemma which confronts us all. First, I will state the problem in the form appropriate to the group at The Institute for Religious and Social Studies. We live in a society which depends on an expanding and developing technology to provide for our ever increasing population an increasingly higher standard of health, comfort, nutrition, and material well-being in general. Our people are willing to work hard for these ends which they consider paramount. Indeed, much of the respect which our country enjoys abroad is based upon our ability in providing ourselves and, in some degree, others with just these amenities of life. This part of our civilization is the principal object of emulation in our way of life for the other people on the earth. This whole trend in our development has a dynamism which cannot be diverted, even were it desirable, and this attitude is expanding over the face of the earth.

A necessary concomitant of this drive to achieve control over natural phenomena for human purpose is the development of weapons of war and destruction. We see two faces of the same coin. As our control over nature becomes greater, as we learn more about the nature of matter and of living things, and apply them to heal and prolong life and health, we acquire new tools for biological warfare. As we learn more of the operation of the human mind, how to heal mental ills, we acquire new tools for the subjugation and degradation of human beings for ignoble ends. In our desire to find new sources of energy to keep the wheels of industry turning in future years, we necessarily develop the capacity of making deadly atomic weapons capable of annihilating millions at one blow.

This two-sidedness of human knowledge is nothing novel. The hand that guides the plow can guide a sword. The gentle voice that gives courage can beguile into evil. What is new is the vastness of the new powers now at hand, the speed with which they can be applied, and the rapid development of even greater powers. Destruction on the vast scale of these weapons is irrevocable. Once applied, society as we know it will be at an end, the future entirely unforeseeable, but certainly our generation would receive no honor from the survivors.

It is not my intention to intensify the pall of fear which now hovers over all mankind. Fear is not a good starting point from which to solve any problem. Nevertheless, this is the time which calls for action rather than lament. Within our own sphere, we must each find some mode of action which will bind men together, give them hope for the future and courage to take the initiative to meet the pressing problems which confront our nation in relation with others. We must emphasize results which come from peace and cooperation, as contrasted with the certain misery which would follow any desperate attempt to settle an issue by force of arms. We must discourage feelings of futility and fatalism which we see expressed all around us. Although we will undoubtedly have to pay a certain price for peace in terms of traditional national sovereignty, future generations will call us blessed, as we do the Founding Fathers of our Republic who gave up the advantages of the extreme form of state rights for the higher values of cooperation for the founding of a new civilization.

That a basis for such cooperation exists in the scientific field was amply demonstrated this summer at the Geneva conference on the peaceful uses of atomic energy. If note is taken, others will find equal opportunity in other spheres to find ways to bring men together for the common welfare of humanity. In spite of all discouragement, it is incumbent on some of us at least, to rise above the cold war kind of thinking of the past decade. We must patiently but persistently seek through action to find ways of turning our fears into hopes. The very things we dread may indeed be the opportunity for our generation to bring the world to paths of enduring peace.

That the world is ready for this was shown by the enormous response in this country, and indeed all over the world, to the faint glimmer of hope which was kindled by the summit conference in Geneva in July, 1955. The conference on the peaceful uses of atomic energy which took place in Geneva the following August demonstrated the feeling in an even more practical way.

I would like to tell you something of this conference because it was something very definite and very specific. It was such an unprecedented event that a little historical background is in order. The suggestion for this conference arose out of President Eisenhower's historic address to the United Nations Assembly, in which he proposed an international agency which would serve as a kind of international pool for nuclear materials and technical information. All member nations could contribute to and draw from this pool under suitable arrangements which are still [January 3, 1956] under study in the United Nations.

This proposal received very favorable comment in the world press at the time. It was, therefore, natural for the United States to suggest a scientific conference to be held in which scientific information could be exchanged in an atmosphere free from propaganda and intrigue.

I had the honor of being appointed chairman of a committee of one to get this project under way. The project had the strong backing of President Eisenhower, the State Department, and of Mr. Lewis L. Strauss, the chairman of the United States Atomic Energy Commission.

To my surprise, the initial reception of this idea by scientists in this country and in Europe which I visited twice, in the summer and fall of 1954, was even less than lukewarm. There was a hopeless feeling that the conference could not succeed; that it would be regarded as a propaganda stunt; that the Soviets would not join; that the papers presented at the conference would be of an inferior quality because of atomic secrecy; and that, in general, more harm than good could come of it.

However, by persistence and persuasion, and by presenting an attractive list of topics, the British, Canadians, and French were won over to the general idea. In December of 1954 the conference proposal was approved in a resolution in the General Assembly of the United Nations by a vote of sixty nations including the Soviets, with none opposed.

What finally resulted was an agenda close to the original United States proposals, which covered twelve days of fifty-six sessions, and a set of rules and procedures which excluded all discussion of a political nature. The items ranged all the way from pure science and physics, chemistry, biology and medicine, through the technology of nuclear power, the use of radio-isotopes in industry, and the economics and organization of a nuclear energy economy.

As soon as it became clear that the conference would indeed be held and under such significant auspices, the whole mood changed. When invitations went out to American scientists to submit papers for the United States Government to present, over 1,000 papers were submitted within a very short time. There was apparently a strong sentiment latent in American scientists for international co-operation, which took this concrete way of expressing itself. Apathy turned to enthusiasm, and the United States finally presented about 500 papers to the conference. Similar attitudes appeared in other countries in different parts of the world, including those within the Soviet orbit.

I would like to give you some impressions of the result of this conference. The atmosphere was amazingly friendly and intimate. The papers, on the whole, were excellent. Even where material was presented which was not new, the richness of the presentations gave one new and integrated perspectives of the technical situation. We learned about Soviet thinking in this field and of the vast scope of their atomic energy enterprise, second only to our own. We met their scientists and found them extremely capable and with the same problems, and, what is more important, with the same attitudes toward science as our own. For the Soviet delegates it was a tremendous experience, for most of them had never been outside of Russia or met Western scientists with whose work they were familiar.

I would like to quote a few paragraphs to you from a talk which was given by one of the Soviet scientists over the Moscow radio, beamed to Hungary, in Hungarian, from a translation which I received. In other words, this is not propaganda aimed at the United States but to Hungary.

The international scientific conference called in Geneva to deliberate on the peaceful uses of atomic energy was not only the first truly great international conference in the field of physics; we can certainly claim as regards scope and significance that it was a conference of scientists unique in history. The circle of topics discussed was very wide, yet it centered on one principal problem: how to turn the vast source of energy latent in the nucleus of the atom more quickly and more productively to the benefit of mankind.

It was of paramount importance that at the great conference an atmosphere was created that was at once friendly, free from superfluous officiousness, and characterized by objectivity worthy of such a serious scientific gathering. At the conference sessions, the debates were very active and friendly in tone which, however, did not preclude critical observation. It is to be noted with satisfaction that the scientists of the world easily found a common language. The significance of this fact is inestimable.

The participants of the conference paid constant and great attention to the contributions of the Soviet delegates. In the course of our conversations, my foreign colleagues repeatedly declared how impressed they were by the new data concerning the construction in the U.S.S.R. of the new accelerator nearing completion. While noting with satisfaction the recognition accorded Soviet science at the Geneva conference, I by no means wish to claim the contributions of scientists from other countries or their exhibitions were less significant or interesting than ours. On the contrary, many were most successful.

Thus, I speak of the subject nearest to me—the accelerators of charged particles. I want first and foremost to point to the outstanding report presented by Ernest Lawrence, the eminent United States expert on high voltage accelerators. Our scientists and engineers were unanimous in their praise of the report of the United States scientist, Dr. Zinn, on the core of the reactor. Most noteworthy were the exhibitions staged by Western countries, the United States exhibition in particular.

To sum up, there were many most valuable and interesting things from all the experts. The conference has given a very great incentive for mutual exchange of views and will undoubtedly promote the more rapid advance of science and technique.

If this speech delivered as propaganda to Hungary is representative of the impressions of the Russian scientists, as I know it is of ours, I am quite satisfied with the results of this conference in reestablishing the worldwide community and communion of scientists. I hope that the spirit which was generated by this conference will have its effects in the future. It shows men separated by political and geographical barriers nevertheless can combine in a common human endeavor, and that the living tradition of science cannot be killed even by two generations of totalitarian oppression.

I am afraid I have departed from the general theme of these meetings by making my own private dilemma a public dilemma. Yet I cannot do otherwise. I have no private problem which begins to compare in urgency and magnitude with the problem I have placed before you as individuals, as members of your various communities, as citizens of the United States, as residents of this globe.

As I have said, I do not believe these problems to be insoluble nor do I believe there is a general grand solution. Only through many different efforts, from many directions will we emerge from the clouded valley into the clear uplands of hope.

Discussion at The Institute for Religious and Social Studies
January 3, 1956

Question: Would Professor Rabi care to comment on a news item in Sunday's *Tribune* about the scientist, Linus Pauling, contradicting the remark of Professor Compton that as he grew older he became more religious?

Professor Rabi: What did you want me to say—support it, refute it, or illuminate it? I don't know what he meant by becoming more religious. My own experience is that as I grow older I find some of the powers I possessed when I was younger dropped off. I don't learn as fast. I can't do arithmetic as rapidly. I find learning some things the second time is more difficult than the first.

On the other hand, one gets an accumulation of experience which, at least in my case, tones down the contrasts that one saw so sharply when one was young. The pastel shades in life come into prominence much more than they were at first. One is more ready to accept various ideas. As for traditional attitudes, one sees other values in them that one did not see in the beginning. In that sense, I think it is quite possible.

Question: Do you think as a result of the Geneva conference, there was produced any deterrent effect on what we have always thought was the purpose or intent of Russia? Then, in the next instance, what attitude would such scientists as Professor Urey and the late Professor Fermi take with regard to this? How quickly could we mobilize the scientific intelligence of this country in case of a sneak attack upon us so we would still have the upper hand?

Professor Rabi: I am very glad you brought up this question. At this time I find myself totally opposed to that view. I do not believe in the years to come—and by this, I don't see a long vista of time, one could almost say in the months to come—that there is such a thing as having the upper hand in the field of nuclear warfare. It is much more a question of whether you are willing to throw all your values, all your possessions, your whole society, your whole set of concepts, your whole organization, all the traditions which have been built up through the centuries—whether you are willing to throw them away or whether you wish to compromise with them and let them develop under conditions where men have not suffered as extremely, where society has not been shaken to its foundations, as it would be even in a small nuclear war.

I picture to myself a situation in the United States where we might have had a war, and after a short period we hear no radio signals out of an enemy country, and we discover that we have destroyed them utterly. And in the process we have destroyed our great cities, our centers of communication; where there isn't a family in the country that hasn't lost some dear ones; where illness is universal; where starvation prevails; where disorganization is complete; where there is no trace of power except in the scattered remnants of the military.

This is the nature of "winning" the nuclear war. I am opposed to the whole concept of thinking of such a war as actually thinkable. Therefore, I call upon you all to put forth your best efforts to get out of this way of thinking—to find ways and means of compromise and adjustment to these new facts, so that we can look to a development in the future, not of shambles, but of what we have now.

Question: Will Professor Rabi tell us what we should do on the question of international control? I would like to accept his point of view, but how are we to get international control if Russia doesn't yield on that?

Professor Rabi: I wish you had asked me an easier one. I have no answer in a specific form. That is the job of our State Department and the people at the top. I do think an attitude of seeking, of trying for this, must exist in the country, so that our statesmen can get moral and political support for their efforts in this direction.

The problem I have presented for our country is not the problem of our country alone. My opposite number sitting in Russia or anywhere else sees the same thing; he sees exactly the same thing. He sees the possibility that whatever they have succeeded in building up after two generations of the hardest kind of work, under conditions of oppression, under conditions of a drive which has never been seen before, he sees the possibility of all this going up in smoke, the state which they hoped to make utterly ruined and going back to a situation, perhaps, of the eighth century, with bands of bandits roaming around, everything they built destroyed. I do not think on the other side they see this matter any more lightly than we do.

For that reason I think there is hope. We have to think about it on that scale, rather than the question of who would win. There is no such thing as winning, as in the sense of winning the past war— whatever comfort we got out of that.

V

BOTH FREE AND BOUND

BY

ALBERT J. PENNER

In dealing with the topic, "Dilemmas and Compromises in the Work of a Protestant Minister," I will necessarily reflect my own position which is that of one who by choice belongs to the liberal, free church, nonconformist tradition. I have never found myself in a difficult situation either with an ecclesiastical superior, or with an ecclesiastical system. I have never felt the pressure to accept or profess a formal creed to which I could not give honest assent.

As a Protestant minister I feel myself to be both free and bound. I am free to speak the truth as I see it. I am bound at the same time to a Christian tradition and to a Gospel. I am the minister of a church and the chosen leader of a congregation. I occupy an office, and my freedom must be exercised within the limitations of that office.

I shall not discuss the predicaments in which a Protestant minister may find himself through his own faults and failures. Examples of this kind, which I might cite, are both humorous and tragic. Rather I shall endeavor to mention some of the dilemmas and compromises which, in my opinion, may be the lot of any minister who is earnest and conscientious, and who seeks to discharge his office faithfully.

1. It seems to me that ministers frequently face dilemmas and are tempted to make compromises because of their social position and economic situation.

Ministers are sometimes spoken of as "men of God." It is an inaccurate and often inappropriate appellation. They are just as human as anyone else. They are supposed to remember constantly that "their citizenship is in heaven" and to forget as much as they can their earthly needs. They are regarded as spiritual leaders and are presumed to have mainly spiritual needs and concerns. Too many churches find this a convenient reason to keep the salary scale low. To keep him poor helps to keep him humble, and poverty and humility keep him devout.

Furthermore, ministers are usually reluctant to ask for more money. There are notable exceptions, of course. Yet a minister ordinarily has a family. He is expected to entertain freely. He and his family are expected to dress well. They are expected to head the list of contributors to the church, and to give to numerous good causes in the community. The children are expected to be exemplars of good breeding. He and his wife have perhaps an above average appreciation of the values of good education and they are resolved that their children shall have the very best.

Here then is the dilemma: there is need to have a measure of economic security and to maintain a certain social position, to dress reasonably well, to send the children to good schools, to buy the necessary books, to give generously, and to own a car. But if these needs are stressed unduly they may display a degree of self-seeking, a preoccupation with worldly standards, an inordinate love of comfort, a lack of modesty, simplicity, and trust.

On the other hand, if these needs are not sufficiently recognized one may be unfair to one's family, one may deny oneself and them experiences and opportunities which are important. One may get a bad community reputation for nonpayment of bills. Or one may come to expect and even seek special treatment, special discounts and favors, which is humiliating and reprehensible. It is possible for a man to compromise his integrity if he feels himself caught in this kind of predicament.

2. The need to be successful often poses dilemmas and calls for compromises. Protestant churches, unfortunately, are often in competitive situations. Many denominational walls are not very high. Baptists, Methodists, Congregationalists, Presbyterians, for example, change denominations with increasing frequency. I am frankly de-

lighted when a Baptist or Methodist or an Episcopalian wishes to join my church. I don't turn him away with the suggestion that he had better find a church of his own denomination. And from the number of former Congregationalists in New York City who belong to other churches I must conclude that all other ministers enjoy this kind of "sheep stealing" as I do.

Our Protestant churches have to be successful in such tangible terms as growing memberships, increasing financial support, improving attendance. They depend upon the free will gifts of the people, and if these are not sufficiently forthcoming the church suffers, the minister suffers, and rumors begin to be heard that "it is time for a change." The minister's future therefore depends upon his ability to lead in a "successful" operation, and that means to make the church a going concern which can balance its budget at the end of the year. In some denominations, such as the Methodist, there is an ecclesiastical organization which can resolve situations involving unhappy churches and ministers, but in most Protestant churches the minister is pretty much on his own. If he is in trouble he can get sympathy, but he can rarely get much else.

In this situation the minister is tempted to yield to the superficial and popular notion of success and to adapt his program and methods to achieving it. He will avoid alienating parishioners, especially if they are people of means. He will keep still about controversial issues about which he ought to speak. He may lower the standards for church membership. He may institute moneyraising schemes which are not above criticism. He is tempted to lose sight of the religious purposes for which the church really exists. He may become so immersed in program and administration that he forgets the people committed to his care.

He may feel that the alternative is to be the minister of a church declining in morale, in membership, in resources, in program, and in the end become disspirited and a failure. At the same time he must avoid putting on a martyr's mantle, and assume that the reason things are not going well is not because of any failure on his part but because of his faithfulness to the Gospel's absolute demands.

In such a situation the minister must endeavor not to sell his soul to the goddess success while maintaining a church that is both outwardly and inwardly strong.

3. Closely related to the temptation to offer too many hostages to success is the temptation for a minister to become a spokesman for the prevailing culture; to become captive to the spirit of the age rather than free to proclaim eternal truth.

Ten or more years ago a famous editorial in *Fortune Magazine* charged that the clergy were merely echoes of the prevailing culture, repeating what they heard "the world" say, rather than "voices" speaking from a higher dimension *to* the world. Here was a business magazine demanding that ministers address themselves *to* the culture, rather than merely echoing the assumptions and prevailing opinions and prejudices of that culture.

The charge is not without foundation. In their study, *Ethics in a Business Society,* Marquis Childs and Douglass Cater document their contention that Christianity tends to become adjusted to capitalist America. Similarly Will Herberg, in his recent sociological study of the American religious scene published under the title *Protestant–Catholic–Jew,* shows how religion for many people has tended to become equated with "the American Way of Life" as that is popularly understood.

It is well known that Protestant churches very frequently tend to draw into their memberships people from the same social and economic strata, sharing similar prejudices and attitudes, and that they often therefore do not represent a fair cross-section of our population.

The current tremendous growth of the suburbs will almost surely strengthen this trend. These new communities by and large are constituted of families from similar economic levels. The new churches will be made up of people whose political, economic, and social outlook is similar, and they will undoubtedly reflect a much narrower point of view than has been true in typical American communities.

In the Bible prosperity was usually regarded as the most evident sign of divine favor. That ancient view may have been repudiated by theologians, but it is still held in great popular esteem—especially by the prosperous.

There is a saying that "he who pays the piper calls the tune." Calling the tune is seldom done in an audible way. I have never had a layman stomp out of church in the middle of a sermon. But there are subtle pressures of which any minister becomes aware. If he knows his members as he should, he will know what they like and especially what they don't like; and he will consciously or unconsciously adapt himself to the prevailing climate.

We ministers like to be liked as well as anybody else. We breathe the same air as anybody else. We, too, are the beneficiaries of our culture. Is it not a strong possibility that some of us should be reluctant to be too critical of that culture, or alas, that we may have lost the ability to see what is evil or idolatrous in it? Or if we have not lost our perceptiveness we are tempted to take to ourselves the advice of Mr. Worldly Wiseman to his son:

> My son, be a reformer, yes
> Your purpose I commend and bless;
> Stand up, speak boldly, do not fear,
> Naught will the world refuse to hear
> Of all that you may have to say
> If phrased in an ambiguous way.

You may talk about brotherhood and peace and race relations and politics and social action, but it's best to keep it very general. It's much safer to be ambiguous than bold, and you can still make yourself and others believe that you're being prophetic.

4. A slightly different predicament faces the minister when he feels he ought to take a position on public issues and run the risk of alienating some of his members. If you do or say nothing, you pussyfoot; if you speak or act, you cause dissension. So one may be tempted "to trim one's moral sails to fit the situational cloth."

Some years ago, in a former parish, I publicly announced my readiness to counsel with Conscientious Objectors. Though not a pacifist myself, I believed, as I still do, in the rights of conscience and I stood prepared to encourage and uphold any young man who had sincere and conscientious convictions against serving in the armed forces. I still have in my files a searing letter from a Superior Court Judge, who was a member of my church, castigating me for my position. I do not recall that he ever attended church again during my pastorate, though I did my best to maintain a good personal relationship with him. I could have kept still. Very few Conscientious Objectors came to see me as a result of my stand. Was it important or right for me to take the stand I did, or was it not worth raising the issue?

A women's club in a certain church invited Margaret Sanger to give a talk to their members on Planned Parenthood. Her coming was announced in the papers. Almost immediately strong pressures were brought to bear against businessmen who were members of that church. A bank was threatened with the loss of important accounts; a merchant was threatened with loss of business. Under these pressures the trustees of the church withdrew permission to hold the meeting in the church. The result was that Miss Sanger, instead of speaking to thirty-five or forty women, most of them either unmarried or beyond childbearing age, spoke to several hundred persons in a Labor Union Hall, and the meeting attracted very wide publicity.

The minister in the church involved acted correctly and courageously. He was not for cancelling the meeting. But I have wondered about my part in this episode. I have wondered whether I ought to have urged that the meeting be transferred to my own church and whether I should have tried to get my trustees and responsible members to support me in this. Believing in the right of a group to hear whoever they wished to invite, should I have sought to make an issue of this? I took no strong public stand, and while I helped to arrange for the meeting that was finally held, I am not particularly proud of my part in this episode.

Or to cite a more recent case, two years ago I associated myself with a number of other clergymen in an attempt to win a commutation of the death sentence for the Rosenbergs. We made it clear that we were not judging the question of guilt or innocence.

Assuming they were guilty, it seemed to us too severe a sentence, and one reflecting the hysteria of that time. It was a futile as well as a most unpopular cause. Why bother? Why stick one's neck out when it doesn't seem to matter, one way or another? Why espouse an unpopular cause when you may jeopardize your place of respect or confidence in the church and community? If one does not take a position one is a coward; if one does one jeopardizes one's position.

5. Or again, in our Protestant tradition a minister is to combine both priestly and prophetic functions. He is a priest, presiding over the rites and ordinances of the church, being the pastor, the shepherd of his people. He is also a prophet, seeking to fulfil the word of Jeremiah, "He that hath my word, let him speak that word faithfully."

How can the two functions be maintained in proper balance? How can one be both a faithful "spokesman for God" and a faithful shepherd of souls? If one likes to thunder from the pulpit and pronounce judgment like an Amos, one may confuse "Thus say I" with "Thus saith the Lord." And if one lives in close relations with one's people one may become a "hail fellow well met" and compromise one's ability to speak for God.

In Protestantism the pulpit is the freest platform in the world. A congregation has a stake in keeping it free, and in according to the minister all the freedom he needs. But the minister, for his part, must recognize his responsibility to preserve the honor and dignity of the pulpit and not to prostitute it for his own ends of fame or prestige or anything else.

One of our great teachers said once that no teacher can stand before a class year after year and refrain from saying more than he knows. Nor can a preacher stand Sunday after Sunday in his pulpit and refrain from saying more than he knows. George Eliot, who I gather abhorred preachers said, "Preachers are the most irresponsible of all talkers." I suspect there is some truth in this charge. We speak from faith to faith. And we must therefore speak with a proper blend of assurance and humility.

This same problem of saying more than he knows confronts a

minister in his pastoral work. He is available for counsel. A person comes to him with an acute personal problem. It is easy to give some quick and glib assurance when he knows there is no easy and simple assurance. How can one comfort an anxious heart that asks, "Why, if we pray in faith and expect our prayers to be answered can we not be sure it will happen?" There is always the temptation to say what people want to hear, and to appear to solve a terribly difficult problem with a little prayer and a little Scripture and a few easy steps. There are innumerable cults which flourish because people want quick and easy and assuring answers. "The cure of souls" is a very demanding and difficult calling which requires patience and understanding and much love. The minister must not be afraid to cry, "Lord I believe, help thou my unbelief."

6. Another predicament centers in what may be called the minister's authority. In our Protestant churches generally responsibility for leadership is shared between clergy and laity. In churches organized on a congregational basis the minister is a member of the congregation and his status is only functionally different from that of the other members. Ordination "provides entry to no priestly caste, bestows no superiority, prerogative or compulsive authority." [1]
Still he has been set aside for leadership. How is he to exercise his prerogative to lead without usurping power? If he exercises too much authority, he is a dictator and doesn't properly train his people to assume leadership responsibility. If he holds back, he becomes subject to the jest, "There go the people, I must follow them, for am I not their leader?"

Ordination involves acceptance of a grave responsibility. A minister is the chosen leader of the flock committed to his charge. He is to lead the congregation in spiritual matters, which I understand to include everything that properly happens in a church. It is his responsibility to see that the main objectives of the church are not lost sight of. Our churches are experiencing rapid growth at the present time. Church membership is increasing at a faster rate than

[1] H. Cunliffe-Jones, *The Congregational Ministry in the Modern World*, Independent Press, London, 1955, p. 16.

population growth. How are these new members to be assimilated?
How are they to gain a sufficient understanding of the church? How
are we to prevent the increasing secularization of our churches of
which Will Herberg writes, "It is this secularism of a religious people, this religiousness in a secularist framework, that constitutes the
problem posed by the contemporary religious situation in America"? [2]
Whatever else is required, there is also needed strong leadership
on the part of the minister, and under his leadership the training of
laymen and women who understand what a church is for and who
can help to keep it true to its central function.

7. Another dilemma involves the minister's responsibility to his own
congregation and the demands that are legitimately made upon his
time and strength by his denomination and by the community. A
minister who is called to a particular church is at the same time a
member of a denomination; he is also one of the religious leaders
of the community, and both have a claim upon him.

If a man confines his entire effort to his own congregation, he is
shirking his duty to the larger church and the community. If he
responds too readily to the outer demands, he may neglect his prior
and major duty. The sin of many a minister is in saying "Yes" to
every demand, so that he does nothing well. What he must do is
so to apportion his time that he does the main thing well, and yet
does not slight his other legitimate and important activities. Most
of our churches want their pastor to be active in church and community affairs, they want him to represent them well, but they also
want him to be a faithful shepherd of his flock.

This demand upon a man's time may take another form: the
minister in his teaching and preaching has constantly to give of
himself. At the peril of his soul he must spend time in Bible study,
meditation, prayer, reading. He cannot neglect his study. On the
other hand he must be a pastor, visiting the members of the congregation, knowing them in their business as well as in their homes.
Some find the study so inviting that they neglect their parish work.
One of these was described as being for "six days invisible and on

[2] Will Herberg, *Protestant-Catholic-Jew*, Doubleday, New York, 1955, p. 15.

the seventh incomprehensible." Others enjoy their parish responsibilities and neglect the hard work which study demands. I recall
a minister whose widow invited me to select some books from his
library. I discovered that he had not bought a new book in twenty
years. He had a garden fine enough to be pictured in "Massachusetts
Beautiful" and everyone loved him as a man. But his preaching was
arid and dull.

No man is freer than a Protestant minister in the use of his time,
and laziness may become one of his besetting sins. It requires resolution and conscientious planning to make wise and fair use of his
time so that he fulfils to the best of his ability all the demands that
may be made upon him.

8. Let me mention one final area in which tensions arise, namely,
between the absoluteness of the Gospel and the relativities of life.

Few Protestant ministers serve under either Canon Law or the
clearly prescribed rules of a church. They must therefore make many
decisions on the basis of their best judgment, and without guidance
from the larger church. A case in point which frequently arises
is the question of the marriage of divorced persons. There is nothing
in the rules of his church to guide him here. He knows that marriage
is a sacred contract, and, ideally, for life. He realizes that marriages
unfortunately often founder and he believes that it is better that
some marriages be dissolved than continued under pretense and
hypocrisy. If he refuses to marry any divorced persons, as the law of
some churches requires, he believes himself to be unfair to some
who ought to be released from their vows, perhaps to realize a truly
sacramental marriage. If he agrees to marry divorced persons, even
if he exercises discretion and care, he may perform the rite and
regret it afterward. It is rather startling to discover, too late, that
couples have withheld vital information or that he is subject to
pressures from unexpected sources. A girl in a former church came
to see me about her marriage to a man who had been twice married
and divorced. I refused her request on the basis that the young man,
having twice failed, seemed a very poor risk, and that she had not
known him long enough. But her father and mother came to see

me and interceded strongly for their daughter begging me to perform the marriage. They liked the young man. They were sure it would work out well, etc., etc. On their plea I reluctantly agreed. I compromised with my better judgment, and I regret that my fears were too well founded.

Another dilemma arises in counselling with a couple in the case of a mixed marriage, say, between a Protestant and a Roman Catholic. Ordinarily one may not favor a mixed marriage, but when a couple comes to consult a clergyman the decision has usually been made. A Protestant may marry a Catholic in a Catholic rectory or church and remain a member in good standing. A Catholic cannot marry a Protestant in a Protestant church or be married by a Protestant minister, and remain in good standing. I must frankly state that a minister resents the situation in which he finds himself when he must counsel one of his own members to agree to marriage in another church, with all the decisions that are involved in it. Not infrequently does he hear the couple say that they have no present intention to honor the promises which they feel they are compelled to make under duress. Sympathizing with their problem he is probably seldom inclined to object to their decision, even though both horns of this dilemma are to him distasteful.

Here then are some of the areas in which a Protestant minister is confronted by dilemmas and compromises. I am sure that I have not exhausted the number or the nature of them. He knows he is the herald of a Gospel which must be brought down to earth, into the marketplace, into the home, and made meaningful and relevant in all situations. He knows that its pure demands are always beyond human fulfilment and that no day passes that he will not need to say "I have left undone things I ought to have done, and I have done things I ought not to have done." Before any of his parishioners he stands in need of "heaven's mercy and help."

VI

THE PROBLEMS OF THE PHYSICIAN

BY

PETER MARSHALL MURRAY, M.D.

The life of a physician offers innumerable occasions when he meets a dilemma. But I think we are more fortunate than those in other callings, because—realizing our limitations—it is sometimes the act of Providence that we take the other horn of the dilemma, because, after all, that may have been the one we should have taken anyway.

Very often our choosing of the other side, of the other task, of the other fork of the road, results in a happy circumstance.

Medicine is a science, but medicine is also an art. Do one without the other, and you are doing only half a job. Any man, no matter how scientific he might be, if he forgets the art of medicine, is not delivering to the patient what the patient deserves: and no matter how artful the man is, if he is not possessed of knowledge of the science of medicine, he, too, is not doing justice to his patient.

The human body is a self-repairing machine. It is the most wondrous thing ever devised. With all the forward progress, and knowledge, the science and art, we have not yet produced anything that will repair itself and keep itself oiled.

But the human body is a self-repairing machine. It is said that in the course of about seven years it almost replaces itself entirely. You can see, when you rub your hand on a cold morning, a few flakes of the outer cells come off; and that is going on all the time in every organ of the body—new cells are being born, moved up, and the old cells that have served their purpose are being discharged But, it is all being done in an orderly way.

(In the early years of my married life I was making a talk and say-

55

ing that the body changes every seven years. Afterward, a lady came up and said to my wife, "You better look out for your husband. He said a man changes every seven years; and you have been married seven years.")

Disease is an alteration of function or structure, and it is important to keep that in mind at this time, now that we are putting more and more emphasis—and rightly so—on psychosomatic aspects of medicine.

In the beginning, a psychosomatic condition has to do with the alteration of the function, and the vital functions of the body are under the control of the involuntary nervous system. You cannot stop your heart from beating; you cannot stop your intestines from digesting food. Those are involuntary actions under the control of the nervous system, and when we get a derangement of those things we have a psychosomatic condition.

It may be caused by worry, and failure to maintain and meet changing conditions in environment, the things which come up and to which we have to adjust every day, after day.

In the beginning, while purely functional, it may set up a chain of changes that may result in organic structural changes. So the person who is highstrung and nervous, the fellow whose wife is always after him, or the wife whose husband always neglects her, is apt to develop something simulating heart disease, or may develop ulcer of the stomach or colitis. People who work under great stress and tension are apt to get those diseases, which, in the beginning, may be purely functional, that is, if the conditions are righted no structural changes may take place. However, if such structural changes take place, you have ulcer, or colitis, or something else. Just as sure as the structural changes or alterations occur—changing your wife or your husband isn't going to help—you are going to have to have an operation.

One famous surgeon in Philadelphia said he never liked to operate on an ulcer until it had been cured by a half dozen medical men.

Those psychosomatic diseases deserve our attention, and as we become more intelligent about the influence of the mind over the body, we can look way down the roadway and see a cloud no bigger than a man's hand, which is apt to result in catastrophe unless we recognize it while it is a little cloud.

I want to confine my remarks to two or three angles of the medical field. I want to say a few words about cancer; and I want to say a few words about syphilis; and I want to say a few words about infertility.

Cancer—in a few words—is simply the misbehavior of body cells, so that you have the makings of cancer in your body already. You don't have to get anything in. You don't import anything, you don't have to get any germ. You can't catch it from anybody.

When your own body cells reproduce themselves, but not after the pattern as set down by an all-wise Providence, where there is structure, and function, and order, but where they fail to obey those fundamental laws of structure and function and order, and begin to multiply without plan or purpose, then, that is cancer. That is all there is to it.

We know a good many things about cancer, but we do not know what the stimulus is that sets off these cells. We know continued irritation or certain conditions which if not corrected, may result in that stimulation of body cells in setting them off so that they will behave in that disorderly fashion.

Cancer has a method of spreading through the lymphatic and circulatory system. It breaks away, and little pieces get into the blood stream. Just as something may get into the water supply here and contaminate the water way down on Forty-second Street. In the body the little pieces break off and lodge themselves sometimes in distant parts of the body, which is what we call metastasis.

So that, then, the behavior of that particular cancer is dependent upon the type of cell which started it in the first place. It may be a cell that multiplies rapidly. It may be a cell at a stage where it is tough, and won't multiply so rapidly. On that basis, we very often decide whether we should use radium or surgery.

I am emphasizing these things to explain how impossible it is to tell in any particular case what is going to happen. It is utterly impossible to tell what is going to happen in a given case, because of the varied manifestations and forms which this condition may take.

Some years ago syphilis was a word we did not use in polite circles. I believe we have inherited a few phobias from that date, since a great many people have suffered untold hardships because it is alleged they have a 4-plus Wassermann, which is one of the tests used in diagnosing syphilis.

It is called a venereal disease; it is associated with immorality. But that is not the only way you can contract syphilis. It is blood-borne after it gets into the system. While it may start at one localized point, it gets into the blood stream, invades the arteries and other organs of the body, and then it obeys certain rules.

It may lie dormant for three or four months, maybe four or five years, maybe longer, and it will break out again. So the various tests are not altogether reliable. They are an index, and the wise doctor takes that as one link in the chain when he is forging a chain of evidence to lay out the prescription for the proper course of treatment. When a patient has a positive Wassermann it may mean he has syphilis, and it may not. If the test is 1, 2, 3, or 4, positive, they mean different things. But in our hysteria, everyone who has a positive Wassermann is syphilitic.

Unless you have an open sore you are in no danger of transmitting the disease. It is impossible to contract syphilis from another person except from an open sore, and a break in the skin. The danger of a person who has a 4-plus Wassermann is to that person himself. Too much emphasis is put on 4-plus Wassermann in avenues of employment.

Now as to infertility. The strongest urge in humankind is to propagate the race. The urge of a mother for her child is one of the strongest urges known to man.

Yet in the field of infertility we often face the dilemma of what we are going to tell a mother or a husband—a marriage may depend on it, or future happiness may depend on it. What then should we do, or not do when we come across a condition where we should say, "You are not going to be a mother," or "You won't become a mother"?

I tell young doctors never to tell a woman she won't become a mother. I have had too many people sit in the chair opposite my desk and say, "The doctor told me I couldn't become a mother; now look at me." So, I tell them that all the signs point to the fact that they cannot become pregnant or that it is not likely that they will. I tell them to think about adoption or some other recourse, but I never tell them point blank, "You cannot become a mother."

In infertility, the matter involves the examination of a couple. The male or the female, or both, are at fault sometimes. It is estimated that in thirty per cent to forty per cent of the cases, it is the male who is infertile. So, you examine both, and you evaluate both, and even then you may not be successful.

So, the function of all treatment and study of these infertile couples is to restore them as nearly as possible to normal, and then hope for the best.

There are a great many areas in which we have to use discretion and judgment. We have to be psychologists; we have to anticipate the effect on the person of what we tell them, and the effect on their mate and on the whole family.

I was reading the other day a volume by Frederick M. Loomis entitled *Consultation Room*.[1] Loomis was a nationally known obstetrician and gynecologist. He had under his care a woman about to become a mother. He found that the baby was in transverse position, and about to be born buttocks first. The death rate in that type of patient is higher than normal. In the beginning of the delivery, he found, by feeling the various parts and how they were behaving, that this child had a congenital deformity which he discovered before it was born.

He pulled down one leg, which was perfectly normal, and when he went to reach for the other leg, he could not find it. Finally, the baby reached a point where he could pull on it a little more, and he discovered the deformity. There was no leg between the thigh and knee, and the legs could never be of equal length.

He had to do rapid-fire calculation—he thought, "If I delay five minutes that baby will never be born alive. It will never breathe. If I deliver it, the poor distraught mother is going to be all torn to pieces emotionally; she will probably waste her life's substance

[1] A. A. Knopf, New York, 1939.

going from orthopedic clinic to orthopedic clinic. What shall I do?"

As he fumbled, he thought nobody will know, not even the nurses, if I delay five minutes. They put a towel over his hand, as is usual, and he felt a vigorous kick by the good leg. And such a vigorous expression of life did something to him. "I will deliver it. I will let God have His way." He delivered the baby, deformed as it was. In the morning he broke the story to the child's mother, and she was heartbroken. She had a rough convalescence, and after going from clinic to clinic she dropped out of his sight.

The next chapter of the story takes place at a Christmas party some twenty years later, in Los Angeles, California. It was a beautiful ceremony, of the nurses marching down the aisle, in Red Cross habiliments. The music was playing and a chorus singing; and then the Christmas tree lighted up, and the lights shone on the curtain as it was drawn back, and there were three beautiful girls, one playing the cello, one the violin, and one playing the harp. He said, "There was something about the girl playing the harp—I always love to hear someone play the harp—but how beautiful she was, and how she seemed to put her whole soul into it." He couldn't take his eyes off her.

At the conclusion of the program a woman he did not recognize came down the aisle to him. She said, "Doctor, I saw you watching that girl. That is your baby. You do not know me, but I am the mother that you delivered of that deformed child. For a long time we did have it rough, but now we have fitted her with an artificial limb, and she can walk and play." Because she was handicapped in her physical exercises, she learned to play the harp; and now she is going to be one of the great harpists of the world.

"There is the answer," he said, and asked her to play "Silent Night" for him. He said, "I have found the answer I have been seeking all these years."

I want to come more to the point and quote with permission of the authors rather copiously from a recent volume entitled *"Should The Patient Know The Truth?"* [2] This volume was put out by Dr. Samuel Standard and Dr. Helmuth Nathan, both of the Syden-

[2] Springer Publishing Company, New York, 1955.

ham Hospital; Standard is also at University Hospital, and Nathan at Einstein Medical College.

It is a remarkable collection of essays and opinions by physicians and nurses and ministers and social workers on ethical and moral questions that are raised when you ask yourself, "Should the patient know the truth?"

I think the fundamental answer lies in that the truth is an instrument of therapy just as much as an injection, because so much of the art of medicine hinges on the confidence which the patient has in the doctor, as well as on the doctor with his knowledge of what is going on. Often the truth, or the withholding of it, or the shaping of it, will determine the patient's reaction in such a way that it may mean life or death to that patient.

There are patients of all different kinds of makeups and motivations and reasons for living, and degrees of integrity and degrees of maturity. You cannot lay down hard and fast rules.

What is it that may make telling the whole truth so brutal? There are few people who will continue to fight, who will continue to be part of life, in the hope they are not forever lost. A shipwrecked sailor who survives the ordeal of drifting on a limitless ocean for days or weeks, owes much of his ability to continue the struggle each day to his abiding faith that rescue will come.

The physician must beware not to break this will to live in his patients. There are few who will continue to live bravely and freely when they know that their end is near. If this quality of strength is found in a patient, the physician will tell him the truth. Yet, because of the very few that possess that strength, one may not create despair and hopelessness in the many not so constituted.

There are religious conditions, economic conditions, family, or business conditions, which make it necessary to inform certain patients, in certain degrees, of their condition. Those duties must be obeyed, following the dictates of your own conscience.

When, however, the patient is nearing the end it is often better for the family to come close to him, and not to continue saying that this is just a passing trouble that will be over. The patient's realization that his family understands his plight will then be found of comfort. By such understanding the family, in effect, says to him: "Yes, we are in difficulty, but we have been in difficulty before, and we will see our way through this one. You are not alone, the family is with you, the whole medical profession is with you, and everything that can be done is being done to make you better."

I have right now, at this moment, a colleague, a college classmate, who is on just such a bed of illness. We thought the end had come last May, but he is still with us, and he is still able to perform some of the vital functions of his office. There are two doctors in attendance, and they represent two different personalities. One doctor says there is no need of employing any heroic methods to help him; you might stop at this. The other doctor says "If it is your wish that we do everything, as long as I can I will stand by you."

You can take your choice between the approaches, ethical, moral, or otherwise, of those two men.

Treatment of a patient does not follow a constant set of rules. As the disease changes, as the patient's faculties change with it, as the family's attitude changes, truths, too, change; and the doctor demonstrates his ability by reacting to the ever new environment.

No doctor will be right each time. He can take advice, he can read about the care of patients in such situations, but he must create in the crucible of his own mind an amalgam of all that information with the person he is. Then, and only then, what comes out of him will be authentic and meaningful to the patient; only then will he have acquired the wisdom needed for dealing with the sick.

Some patients show through their behavior, through interest in their drugs and treatments, through their plans and preoccupations, that they don't want to be told, though the knowledge of their condition may be close to the surface of consciousness. That way, they may feel, they are best able to preserve equilibrium. To force any knowledge, not demanded or not clearly demanded, upon such a person will be an unkind, insensitive act.

As Willard L. Sperry says: "Speaking the truth in love may mean, at times, keeping silence."

That is especially the case with the patient who has cancer. The very word seems to spell terror and doom for many people, and is avoided. Words like tumor, swelling, lump or growth, and sometimes even sarcoma, the deeper but, to the laity, less known form of cancer, are used as substitutes.

In this light, the question, "Should the patient know the truth?" changes to the challenge, "Am I ready and willing to be with the patient on his last road, willing to accept his feelings, different as they might be from mine, willing to respect equally his wish to be told or to be spared?" Only when we are free for both, is it true as Walt Whitman says: "The faithful hand of the living does not desert the hand of the dying."

What, after all, is this truth which we can hide or give? It is conditioned by the limits of our knowledge and ability; it may change not only with the changing and increasing proficiency of medical science, but also with unexpected and unforeseeable turns in the natural course of diseases.

If the physician realized that all his truthfulness does not empower him to pronounce ultimate and inescapable sentences, and if the patient recognizes that the physician's answer is not a final judgment, then the confidence between the physician and patient will not be overtaxed when the truth is told.

Yes, there are circumstances, there are people, there are times, that make fixed rules of conduct, moral, ethical, or even religious, a rather debatable quality. When such a moment comes, an understanding of the conditions should guide a man to break the rule for the greater good—to save the patient first, and paste together the fragments of one's shattered conscience at a later date.

These are the risks we must all take with our soul. Robert Frost, in his short poem "Bravado," [3] says it most simply:

> Have I not walked without an upward look
> Of caution under stars that very well
> Might not have missed me when they shot and fell?
> It was a risk I had to take—and took.

[3] *Complete Poems of Robert Frost 1949*, Henry Holt & Company, New York, 1949, p. 531.

VII

THE RABBI MEETS SOME BIG DILEMMAS

BY

JULIUS MARK

The dictionary definition of the word compromise is "a settlement of differences by mutual concessions" or "the adjustment of conflicting claims through arbitration." In this sense the willingness to compromise is essential to the creation of friendly relations among human beings and the establishment of peace among nations. "All association must be a compromise," wrote Emerson in his essay on friendship, a thought which Edmund Burke had expressed in his famous speech on "Conciliation with America" when he declared that "all government—indeed, every human benefit and enjoyment, every virtue and every prudent act—is founded on compromise and barter."

The need for compromise, resulting from a willingness to give as well as take, is evident in every human relationship. Many a marriage founders upon the rocks of self-righteousness and uncompromising obstinacy. Friendship is impossible except among men who yield graciously to one another's interests and desires, as well as expect a mutual appreciation of views and mutual respect for personalities. A business transaction which enriches one of the interested parties and impoverishes the other can make only for hatred and hostility. Many a war would have been prevented, including the American Revolutionary struggle, if Burke's sane plea for compromise, many times repeated by Lincoln before the outbreak of the Civil War, had not fallen upon deaf ears. The heartbreaking conflict that is inflaming the Near East at the present moment [November, 1955] can unquestionably be settled upon the basis of compromise, if wholeheartedly entered into by both sides.

65

Thus, in the area of international relations even as in the relations between individuals, mutual understanding and peace are founded upon a willingness to reconcile differences and to adjust divergences and disagreements. "From day to day," writes Edmond Cahn in *The Moral Decision,* "our experiences remind us that we cannot make a moral decision without sacrificing at least a part of one desire for another." It is, in fact, a mark of maturity to practice the arts of accommodation.

The word compromise assumes a far different connotation, however, when one side or the other remains unbending and inflexible. A husband or wife who demands all and gives nothing in return will either destroy the marriage or, if the union is not severed, will reduce his or her spouse to a state of abject servility and destroy his or her self-respect. Divorce is evil, but sometimes there is no other way out. War is evil, but nations have resorted to violence as the lesser evil when peace can be purchased only at the price of dishonor or self-immolation. Israel has offered to compensate the Arab refugees for their lost lands and property, permit her neighbors routes through her territory, make available the port of Haifa to Jordan which enjoys no port facilities, and even allow some of the refugees to return, but she refuses to compromise to the extent of accepting them all or giving up any of her already truncated territory, since that could well mean national suicide. When compromise means the extinction of one's most precious values—such as political independence, moral freedom, or religious conviction —the only outcome is the undermining of self-respect and the subversion of the human personality. Far better was Mattathias's counsel to his handful of followers that they show themselves men in behalf of the Torah.

Into the life of every human being who is sensitive to moral values there come dilemmas which require resolution. In most instances, I dare say, it is a question of adjustment to other individuals when compromises of a less serious nature must and should be made in order to advance and perfect human fellowship. In other cases there may arise a situation so grave that an agonized decision must be made. The mettle of a man's character is frequently gauged, par ticularly in times of tension and suspicion, by the manner in which he reacts in such a crisis. A courageous refusal to compromise with his principles may cost him his livelihood, his freedom, or even his life. On the other hand, if he permits himself to be dissuaded from taking a stand by family, friends, or his own timidity and fear, he may suffer the overwhelming loss of his own moral dignity and self-respect.

The dilemma which confronts a man who must make a moral decision becomes more serious when the individual is a minister of religion, since the clergyman, more than any other person, is expected to represent the very embodiment of conscience. He is the champion of God, the guardian of religious idealism, the teacher of righteousness and justice who must never be lacking in the courage to denounce injustice, to defend individuals wrongly accused, and to espouse with forthrightness worthy causes which are unpopular. He does not find this easy. It appears to be characteristic of human nature to glorify dead prophets while stoning the live ones. Furthermore, the ancient prophets received no emoluments from their congregations nor did they appear to be concerned overmuch as to how their families were to be provided for. It is no wonder, therefore, that some ministers should find comfort for their moral ambivalence by castigating for their sins not the modern, but the ancient Egyptians, and seeming to be unaware of the existence of a prophet, Nathan by name, who stood in the presence of the king, pointed directly at him and cried out in the hearing of all: "Thou art the man!"

If the path is stony for the minister of religion who, in these times particularly, finds it difficult not to compromise with his principles, how empty of roses is the path of the rabbi! It has been said that a Jew is like everyone else—except more so! In the same manner, we may describe a rabbi as a man who is like any minister of religion, but more so. For the rabbi is not only confronted with the same moral dilemmas which face his colleagues of other faiths, but in addition is a spiritual leader among a people that has been subjected to shameful suffering at the hands of their fellow men and is still more or less generally misunderstood. One of the results has been that Jews have become keenly sensitive to public opinion. Many object strenuously to their fellow Jews publicly speaking for causes, because in the minds of some these causes are controversial. That they may be righteous causes is beside the point. Jews are concerned with the "good name" of their people, a reputation which they believe they can win and perpetuate by following a policy of self-abnegation and self-effacement. Rabbis who find the noblest interpretation of Judaism in Micah's glowing definition of God's requirements of man as embracing the doing of justice, loving of mercy, and walking in humility before God, and who would apply these glorious teachings to every human relationship, are sometimes accused of meddling in politics. A rabbi recently expressed both amusement and sadness when he learned that a member of his congregation objected most vigorously to a passage in a Yom Kippur sermon in which he referred to the brutal murder of a young Negro in Mississippi. The man objected on the grounds that his rabbi "had no business mentioning politics" in his sermon. The pulpit of this rabbi, by the way, is not in Mississippi or anywhere in the South, but in enlightened California.

To me it appears that whether rabbis are or are not going to be confronted with moral and the frequently heartbreaking decisions as to when or whether they should speak or be silent—there is a time to be silent even for those who speak—depends very largely upon how they conceive of religion. Is religion a way of looking at certain things or is it a certain way of looking at all things? To some, religion either by definition or, more meaningfully, by the way they react to life's problems, is a way of looking at certain things. To them religion's sole function is to be concerned with such matters as God, prayer, observance of Holy Days and festivals, immortality, repentance, sin, dietary laws, and so forth. They maintain that areas such as business, industry, labor, politics, slums, education, child labor, social security, civil rights, social justice, and so forth are all outside the purview of religion. They would agree with the nineteenth century statesman who said, "Things have come to a pretty pass if religion is going to interfere with private life." I dare say that many Reform rabbis would be in agreement with their Orthodox brethren on this estimate of religion—with the possible exception of omitting the dietary laws.

Religion, does, to be sure, concern itself with God, prayer, and so forth, but to other rabbis, important though these are, they by no means constitute the totality of Judaism or of religion. To them religion in its truest sense is a certain way, based upon the awareness of God, of looking at *all* things. It is religion with the Prophetic impact—religion not so much as a vehicle for chaperoning souls to heaven, but as a challenge to man to create a little more heaven on earth. That is why the Prophets, deriving their authority from God, preached against corrupt politics, land monopoly, social injustice, racial bigotry, national arrogance, and war. Amos could well understand the timid and cautious of our own times, which were probably like his own, when he declared: "Therefore the prudent doth keep silent in such a time, for it is an evil time" (Amos 5.13).

The function of the rabbinate, as is well known, has changed with the passing of the years and centuries, even as Jewish life has changed. There was a time—and there are some rabbis who maintain the tradition to this day—when the rabbi was the scholar, the judge, the expert who was called upon to decide questions of ritual. His duties even in Synagogue were few and hardly time consuming, since these were performed for the most part by other functionaries. His preaching, limited to several times in the year, was devoted to the interpretation and exposition of obscure points of law. Frequently he was hardly concerned with what went on in the outer world, since his chief delight was in the study of Torah. He kept the flame of Jewish scholarship burning. In the truest sense, he was a disciple of Jochanan Ben Zachai who was infinitely more successful in perpetuating the Jewish people and the Jewish faith than were the defenders of Jerusalem against the might of Rome.

There is still a place for rabbis of this type, but they usually are not spiritual leaders of congregations, but faculty members of theological seminaries or teachers in *Yeshivoth*. The average rabbi of today could not even if he wished—though there are exceptions—find more than a minimal amount of time for scholarship. The demands made upon his time to render a thousand services to his people and community are many and burdensome. He preaches not twice a year, but twice a week—a service which he is expected to perform even by those who worship only twice a year. He conducts an educational program comprising all age-groups from nursery school through adulthood. He must work with a multiplicity of organizations within his congregation—women's societies, men's clubs, young people's groups. He is expected to be a pastor and make frequent calls on his people—the healthy as well as the sick. He officiates at weddings and funerals. He participates in community activities—general as well as Jewish—Red Cross, Boy Scouts, Service Clubs, as well as B'nai B'rith, Zionist Organization of America, United Jewish Appeal, Joint Defense Appeal, Jewish Welfare Board, American Jewish Committee, and American Jewish Congress. He makes frequent addresses before nonSynagogue organizations, including schools, colleges, meetings and conventions of all kinds. He helps to administer the affairs of his congregation, persuading nonmembers to join and assisting his Board of Trustees to meet the congregational budget.

The functions of the modern rabbinate have changed, of course, because Jewish life has changed. Jews are no longer a separate entity, living a separate life apart from the community at large. They are in the community and of the community. They enjoy rights which their fathers living in the ghettos of Europe could hardly have imagined. At the same time, they have responsibilities which a former generation could hardly have been expected to assume. Except for the extremist Orthodox groups in modern Jewish life which have remained inflexible in their resistance to change of any kind, religiously minded Jews who recognize the necessity of coming to terms with a changing world have been confronted with dilemmas which change always imposes. Upon the rabbi, as the shepherd of his flock, falls the major responsibility of determining, often against powerful opposition, whether the road along which he is leading his people will make Judaism a more vital, more dynamic, more meaningful influence in their lives, or whether he is directing their steps along a blind alley to futility and frustration. Rabbis themselves are not always agreed on which course is the proper one to pursue, a condition which makes the task of the individual rabbi infinitely more difficult.

There are two areas particularly which try the hearts of rabbis who are willing to compromise in nonessentials, but insist upon standing their ground on questions wherein they are convinced conscience is involved. The one has to do with matters of ritual and the other with the question of the rabbi's right—as well as duty— to interpret Judaism as a certain way of looking at all things. In both areas rabbis who have courageously taken a stand have lost their pulpits—a contingency which they must expect—or, having compromised with principle, live lives of indescribable unhappiness and helpless frustration.

It is well known that in some congregations, heretofore traditionally Orthodox, attempts are being made—sometimes successfully—to introduce the custom, prevalent in Conservative and Reform congregations, of the sexes worshipping together or at least removing the screen or curtain separating them. This is a serious matter for a rabbi who is convinced that such a practice is a subversion of his interpretation of Judaism. If, in spite of his pleading, the majority of the congregation votes in favor of the new practice, there remains for him the one alternative of resigning—even though this step may entail hardship for himself and his family. There is always the possibility, of course, of a split in the congregation on this issue, with the rabbi continuing to serve those who had opposed the change. This outcome is not altogether an unhappy one, since many a new congregation has been formed in just this way.

The Reform rabbi may also find himself in a similar position, sometimes because of his desire to abolish certain rituals because of his conviction that they are outmoded and at other times because he is determined to restore them after they had been abolished. The experiences of two Reform rabbis may serve as illustrations. In 1850, Isaac M. Wise, the brilliant organizer of the American Reform movement, was serving in Albany as rabbi in a congregation which might today be denominated as Conservative. Because on *Rosh Hashonah* of that year he dared to advocate reforms which were distasteful to many of his hearers, especially the president, the latter rose from his seat and on this sacred Jewish festival in the presence of the congregation, struck Rabbi Wise in the face. A riot ensued, the police were called and part of the membership seceded with Rabbi Wise and a new congregation was formed in time for *Yom Kippur* services ten days later. It was the only way that this conflict could be resolved. Both for Wise and the president, as well as their followers, it was simply impossible to compromise.

One of the truly prophetic figures in modern Jewish life was the first chancellor of the Hebrew University, the late Judah L. Magnes. He was a man of brilliant mind, independent thought, impeccable integrity, and unyieldingly courageous in his nonconformity, who cherished above all the sacredness of the human personality. There were times in his life when the masses followed him. At other times they rejected him. But I doubt whether any decent person ever hated Magnes, the purity of whose spirit and the doggedness of whose devotion to principle won him universal respect. He was a Jewish nationalist, but not a chauvinist. He believed in the development of Jewish life in Palestine, but did not consider the establishment of a Jewish political state essential to the realization of the Zionist dream. He fought against the partition of Palestine to the end, even when it was apparent that neither the Arabs nor the Jews approved of his plan for a binational state. But his motives were always lofty and noble. With all his heart he believed in peace—but the only kind of peace that is real—peace founded on justice for all human beings, whatever be their race, creed, or nationality. He was not successful in his long and heroic struggle, but the justice for which he pleaded must become the foundation upon which peaceful human and international relations can be constructed.

For some four years, Magnes was rabbi of the congregation which I have the honor of serving. He accepted the pulpit in 1906, with the explicit stipulation that he would have the right to give free and untrammeled expression to his convictions. He made it clear, at the same time, that if the congregation signified its disagreement with his opinions, he would be at liberty to sever his relations with the congregation whenever he found himself unable to reconcile his views with those to which the congregation adhered. This was a fair enough compact into which a self-respecting rabbi could enter.

During Passover of 1910, Magnes preached a sermon during the course of which he made certain demands which, if not complied with, would result in his resignation. These demands were, first, that *Bar Mitzvah* be restored in Congregation Emanu-El; second, that the study of Hebrew be reintroduced in the religious school; third, that adult classes for the study of Hebrew, Jewish literature, and Jewish history be made part of the congregation's program; fourth, that membership dues be reduced to as low as five dollars per annum; and, fifth, that the traditional prayerbook be substituted for the *Union Prayer Book* at worship.

These conditions the congregation was unable to accept and Magnes's services as Rabbi in Congregation Emanu-El came to a close on October First of that year. It was the only possible outcome in a situation wherein the congregation refuses to be guided by the demands of its Rabbi. It was not a question, mind you, of the freedom of the pulpit. The right of Magnes to advocate his views, whatever they might have been—whether or not the congregation agreed with them—was not under discussion.

The second area in which the modern rabbi is frequently faced with the dilemma of compromising or refusing to compromise what he regards are his principles, concerns his right to interpret Judaism as a certain way of looking at all things. In his view nothing, but nothing human is alien to Judaism, whether it be labor-employer relations, civil rights, race relations, war and peace, or what not. In the exercise of his right, as a teacher of Judaism, to denounce not only evil but evil doers and to speak forthrightly in defense of those who, for whatever reason or (better) excuse, are denied the elemental rights that belong to all human beings, the rabbi is likely to share the experience of Amos who was told in so many words by Amoziah: "Go, peddle your radicalism somewhere else, where the overhead isn't so high." In the minds of many laymen—and some rabbis— there is a dichotomy between religion and life. They say, let the rabbis confine themselves to purely "religious" matters, which have little or nothing to do with the practical affairs of the world. And rabbis, unless they have succeeded in training their congregations over a long period of time to cultivate the Prophetic concept of Judaism, will often discover—in a time of emergency—that they will have to take the consequences.

The most noteworthy exponent of Prophetic preaching among the rabbis of our time was, of course, the late Stephen S. Wise. A man of exceptional gifts of mind, heart, and spirit, and a courageous and dedicated servant of his people, an orator of tremendous power and persuasiveness, Wise carried on a lifelong battle for freedom of the pulpit, which he interpreted as the rabbi's right to interpret Judaism in accordance with his convictions. To him this meant the application of Prophetic teachings to every human relationship, a conviction which cost him the pulpit of Temple Emanu-El—but which settled once and for all the question of pulpit freedom in that congregation, and encouraged ministers of all faiths to demand the self-same privilege. Like the Prophets of old, Wise was adored by many, particularly among the masses, and detested by others, especially among the powerful and defenders of the *status quo*. He knew that he would have to take the consequences of his audacity for challenging, in the name of the God of Justice, those who were "at ease in Zion," but he never flinched.

There was the dramatic incident—and the repercussions he knew would follow—which occurred in the fall of 1919. Because their demands for a living wage, reasonable working hours, and the right to organize were denied them by the United States Steel Corporation, a strike had been called by the employees. Excesses of unbelievable viciousness, including violence against women and children, the corruption of local public officials, the employment of goon squads, were the order of the day. The strikers and those who sympathized with them were labeled "Bolshevists," a dirty word in that period which was applied to all nonconformists. The church and the press were indifferent. Wise felt himself duty and conscience-bound to announce as his theme at a Sunday morning service in Carnegie Hall, "Who are the Bolshevists at Home and Abroad—How Shall We Know Them?"

Wise knew only too well that he would have to pay a heavy price for his daring. Before appearing in his pulpit, he remarked rather sadly to his wonderful and equally courageous wife: "My sermon this morning will light a million dollar blaze." He then explained to her that the congregation was in the process of raising funds for a Synagogue, which was to cost more than a million dollars. He predicted that large gifts would be cancelled as the result of his sermon, a prediction that was fully realized.

In opening his address, he frankly declared that some of the members would refuse to lend their support to the building of the Synagogue because of what he was about to say, but he wanted to make it clear that while it might not be necessary to have a Synagogue, it was necessary for him to speak the truth as he saw the truth on all issues. His sermon having been fully reported in the press, he became the center of a heated and an emotional controversy of massive proportions. While hundreds of letters of approval from men whom he respected reached him, thousands roundly denounced him for "mixing politics with religion," aiding and abetting the radical elements in the country, and bringing the Synagogue and the Jew into disrepute. Resignations from his congregation began to pour in. With bitter irony he observed that "one special type of piety I uniformly evoked from the membership of the Free Synagogue was the piety of resignation."

The resignations having become so numerous, Wise did what any self-respecting minister of religion should do under the circumstances. He offered his own resignation to the executive council of the congregation. After due deliberation, the council refused to accept it, making it clear at the same time that the pulpit of the Free Synagogue was and would remain free, but the Rabbi speaks not for the congregation, but *to* the congregation. The distinction is important. The rabbi, so long as he occupies a pulpit, must be free to express his convictions. The congregation may, or may not, agree with his views and, if it so desires, may ask for his resignation. But so long as he occupies that pulpit, his right to preach the truth as he sees the truth must not be interdicted.

The sequel to the story may be of interest. This particular strike was lost, but the people of this country had become so aroused by the injustices that had been perpetrated that the corporation was to introduce the very reforms it had denied. And Wise never lived to enter the Synagogue—now named after him—which he lost in 1919, but like Moses who was not destined to set foot upon the promised land to which he had led his people, he was called to the Academy on High when God determined that his herculean labors on earth had been completed. Until the day of his death, Wise refused to compromise with what he believed to be evil.

There is another rabbi, not nearly as well known as Wise, of whom I should like to write before concluding. He does not possess the remarkable gifts which belonged to Wise—save one. He is not distinguished for his scholarship, organizing ability, or exceptional oratorical power, but is a dedicated man with infinite courage. His name is Samuel S. Mayerberg, and he is the occupant of a pulpit in Kansas City, Missouri.

Mayerberg is not a belligerent man. On the contrary, his is a tranquil, amicable spirit devoted to the ways of peace. He is known for his profound spirituality and for a ministry that may be described as unusually personal. He is close to his congregation, which is strongly bound to him by ties of mutual affection and love. He would be the last among our colleagues whom we might expect to become the center of a massive civic maelstrom.

Twenty and more years ago Kansas City was in the grip of a thoroughly corrupt political machine which, with the help of the most vicious and unconscionable type of gangster organization, was strangling one of the finest cities of our country. The people were terrified. "The prudent were silent." Church and Synagogue looked the other way. One man, however—a kindly, peaceloving man at that—became so aroused over the shameful situation that he was determined, come what may, to take up the cudgels for civic righteousness, which involved the destruction of one of the most powerful and most deeply entrenched political machines of our times. It was David, armed with stones, fighting a Goliath, cruel, leering, contemptuous, heavily fortified with armament and weapons of steel.

The remarkable thing is that Mayerberg was successful in his battle. But what heartaches and heartbreaks he suffered before the decent people of Kansas City mustered sufficient courage to join him in the bitter struggle! He was constantly threatened by the underworld. On one occasion the car which he was driving was forced against the curb by a cab and a shot was fired. The coroner of Missouri insisted on having heavily armed guards accompany him wherever he went—at services in the Synagogue, at meetings, at weddings, at funerals. He feared for his own life, but even more for the well-being of his wife. Pressure was brought to bear upon his congregation to silence this troublemaker, who was not attending to the duties for which he was engaged. Many members resigned. Some visited him privately to tell him that they believed in his cause, but that it was useless to carry on the fight. They pleaded with him to desist. One member reported that the assessment on a building he owned would be raised from $25,000 to $150,000 if he didn't resign. "I repeat without exaggerated emphasis," he writes, "that one of the greatest hardships in my campaign emanated from decent people who had been recipients of political favors or were under friendly obligation to machine despots." The resignation of dozens of members affected the financial condition of the congregation so seriously that he requested his board of trustees to subtract from his salary any financial loss that was sustained from his activities. Mayerberg literally followed the counsel of Hillel: "In a place where there are no men, strive thou to be a man."

It is not incumbent upon all rabbis, to be sure, to engage in activities which make them the center of controversy. It is quite possible that not timidity, but conviction as to their proper functions in the rabbinate impels them to limit their interests to congregational activities in the narrow sense. It is also a question of the individual's temperament. I assume that some rabbis—as some ministers of other faiths—can serve congregations in Mississippi and not feel it incumbent upon them to cry out with Amos: "Are ye not as the children of the Ethiopians unto Me, O Children of Israel? saith the Lord," when fifty-three Negroes in Yazoo City have been deprived of any opportunity to earn a livelihood, because they petitioned the local Board of Education to admit their children to the white school. The bank will have no dealings with them, the wholesalers refuse to sell any goods to the two or three retailers among them, no one will employ them.

If a rabbi living not in New York, but in Mississippi, demands that the injustice be righted, he may expect every indignity to be heaped upon him and to share the terrifying experience of the scholarly and courageous David Einhorn who, because of his uncompromising opposition to slavery, fled for his life from Baltimore in the dead of night on April 22, 1861. For a rabbi, worthy of the name, will not be swerved from his course by the blandishments of even sincere friends, by threats of bodily harm, or by the fears of self-appointed guardians of Israel's good name. He will be of the disciples of Aaron, loving peace and pursuing it, loving all his fellow creatures, but he will never compromise with his conscience nor follow a multitude engaged in doing evil. He can expect few rewards save only that which is derived from the firm and deepseated conviction that he is performing the will of God.

VIII

AN ANTHROPOLOGIST LEARNS FROM THE HOPI

BY

DOROTHY D. LEE

When I began considering my experiences in order to find
dilemmas for the subject of this paper, every dilemma I found turned
out, after I looked at it carefully, not to have been an actual
dilemma at all. In every case, when I looked at the situation, I
saw very clearly that there was one way that I simply could not
go, and another way which was the only way I could go. So that
each time I searched for my dilemmas, they turned out to be
problematic situations, for which I did not have to compromise
but which I could proceed to solve.

Eventually I decided to choose such a situation and present it to
you, in order to show what made it problematic, what alternatives
it posed, what were the basic principles which were involved and
what kind of thinking I had to do to solve the situation.

I am of Greek origin. I came to this country as a foreign student,
eventually married an American and I am now bringing up four
children who, of course, are not only American citizens but are
potentially all Presidents of the United States—a tremendous responsibility for a mother. I mention this autobiographical item,
because it was to some extent responsible for getting me into the
situation which I want to discuss. I am constantly aware of the fact
that the only upbringing I have experienced immediately is Greek,
whereas I am bringing up four American citizens who must feel
American, think American, and relate themselves in an American
way, not a Greek way.

My husband and I raised our children according to principles
which we shared. One of these was that the self should never be

conceived as an isolate, nor as the focus of the universe, but rather that it should be defined as a social self. We valued society. We believed that only through society could the self grow, be enriched, find strength. We believed to a large extent in what MacIver calls "community"—in the *"Gemeinschaft."* However, we became increasingly aware of the fact that our children were very much individuals, that they liked to make their own choices and decisions. They did not like to conform to the standards of a group, and in fact they did not enjoy groups. They did not seek out gangs of children of their own age. They did not classify according to age; they liked "people," and were given to referring to other children as "people." They enjoyed groups only when these were based on individual friendships binding person to person. They preferred to choose one or two friends, and develop a deep and growing relationship.

The one group which they completely enjoyed, in which they were completely involved, was the family. But that was not a group to them; that just happened to them; it was not a group they went out to join, but one that just grew. They had taken no steps to create such a group. Within the family they did not seem to seek individual independent behavior or choice which went counter to the ends of the family. But when it came to joining organizations such as the Scouts, they all turned away. And this reluctance to see meaning in organized groups with organization and a purpose seemed completely unAmerican.

I did not worry about all this while my husband, who came from generations of Americans, was with me to carry the burden of making the children into good Americans. But when I was left to bring up the children alone, I felt the need to go against the family-centered upbringing of the culture of my birth, so as to "socialize" my children in the American way. I was afraid that, falling between two stools, my children would grow into isolated individuals, cut off from all social nourishment. And I believed in society, as a person and as an anthropologist. Among the primitive societies I studied, I found people who were rich in human quality, poised, strong, true, unique, people who grew from birth until death; and these

were people who had social selves, who lived in societies where individual ends and social ends coincided.

It was while I was considering this problem that I was offered an
opportunity to move to the Middle West, to a city where there was
much concern over group development and group participation;
where group awareness and participation was being implemented
at all levels in the schools. It seemed to offer the solution I was
looking for. We moved. The children were unhappy at school, but
I tried to help them to acquiesce to the new system, to understand
its principles, to adjust to a groupcentered environment. But, since
my working hours coincided with school hours, I had no direct
experience of what went on until the Parents' Open Night before
Thanksgiving.

I went first of all to my son's room, the seventh grade. The
teacher showed me a mural, covering all the walls, depicting the
life of the ancient Egyptians. It was a group project; and the teacher
pointed out the part for which my son was responsible. The painting depicted a war scene: some pinkish, sleek, placid, fat, lifeless
horses. These were nothing like my son's skinny, elongated beasts,
full of straining movement and savage life. I protested that this
could not be my son's doing. The teacher explained that my son
had not been allowed to paint his own unique horses; they were too
different. Since this was a group project, uniformity was essential,
so the children had all copied illustrations from a history textbook.
As I turned away, appalled and only half-convinced, I spotted the
tiny figure of a bird, of no known genus, scraggy, leering, menacing,
and I knew that my son's uniqueness had not been entirely mowed
down in the drive for uniformity; it had burst through, however
irrelevantly and illicitly. It reminded me of the mushrooms which
push up a cement pavement, cracking and disrupting its even
surface; I was happy to see it.

Disturbed at this interpretation of the concept of the group, I
went to the classroom of my daughter who was in the fourth grade
The teacher pointed to a frieze of Pilgrims and Indians in profile
that ran around the wall of the room, and obviously waited for my
admiring response. All the Pilgrims were alike, all the Indians

alike without deviation; alike in size and shape and color. I did not know what I was expected to admire, and finally asked whether the children had pasted up the frieze. The teacher explained that they not only had pasted it, they had actually made it, as a group project. "It was hard to make all the heads alike," she said. "When the children first painted the pictures they all looked different, so we had to throw them away. And then I made an Indian profile and a Pilgrim profile; I wrote directions for coloring each part, and the children traced them and cut out their own. And now they make *one* frieze."

I had another daughter in the tenth grade in high school; and soon after this sad night, her grade decided to have a bake sale to help raise money for the trip they were to take to Washington in their senior year. This did seem like good group participation. The trip was to be a truly cooperative venture, since all the students in the class were working toward it, though not all would manage to go eventually. This time each student was asked to bring cake or cookies for the sale. My daughter took this seriously, and was using it as a learning opportunity. She stayed up late making four batches of cookies for which I contributed the ingredients. She found out the cost of the ingredients, and priced the cookies, adding an appropriate amount for her skilled labor. When she took them to school, she discovered that this was not what had been expected of her. Half the children had asked their mothers to bake for them, and most of the rest had bought baked goods at the corner bakery. Mary's cookies were priced below the cost of the raw materials, as were all the other goods, to make sure that they would sell; yet the students were congratulated on raising all this money for their trip through their own exertions. Mary, concerned over what seemed hypocrisy, decided that the work of the students in selling the cookies would represent their involvement, their share in the raising of funds. But when the time came to sell, the homeroom teacher was there to sell. The teenagers could not be trusted to make change. True, they were studying geometry, but they might make a mistake in subtraction; and besides they might yield to temptation. The group—through its representative, the homeroom teacher—could not expose itself to the fallibility of its members; it could not take a chance on the integrity or the ability of its constituent members. In the interest of insuring good results for the group project, all the strivings of the individual self had to be suppressed.

This is what I found in my children's schools. Was this the end of my search for true group experience? Was this the meaning of the self in society? I saw here not nourishment and enrichment, but impoverishment and diminution of the self. The group here demanded the sacrifice of the very generative force of the self, the vitality, the vagary, the spontaneity. It was superimposed upon the self as an external standard, and could be sustained only through a Procrustean conformity. In these schools the children were not people, not individual persons with integrity peculiar to each. Their being did not call forth respect. What was demanded of them was to form a class based on undeviating similarity; and to achieve this, the striving of the self had to be throttled. Only through destruction of the self could the group thrive.

I was not convinced that this was necessary to the creation of a group. In my study of other people, I had come across societies where the group was far more permeating in the life of the individual, where even the private thoughts and feelings of individuals affected the group. I had studied the Hopi where each person had unique significance, where the people were spontaneous, vital, free, strong. So I went back to a consideration of the Hopi, to find out what there was about their culture which made it possible for an individual to maintain uniqueness and significance within the group structure.

Whatever I say here about the Hopi refers to them as they have been until recently. Change has been going on, and particularly since the past war, when many Hopi went out, either with the armed forces, or to factories, and became more and more exposed to our ways of arranging things, to our way of life. If I use what seems to be the present tense, I use it in its reference to the timeless; and what I say about the Hopi refers to their timeless philosophy of life, to what they call the Hopi way—the good, the right path; only when I give specific examples, do I speak of the actual events of time and space.

The Hopi are Pueblo Indians, living in Arizona. They reckon descent through the mother, and houses belong to the women of the lineage, where their husbands come to join them. In the older villages, the closely related women—sisters, mothers and daughters, aunts and cousins—with their families, occupied one or more adjacent households, where the work of living goes on cooperatively. The men herd, farm, hunt, collect fuel, perhaps spin and weave; the women cooperate in preparing food for the group, caring for young children and for the house, hauling water, making pottery and baskets. And when I say men and women I include boys and girls, who from an early age have the right to work alongside the adults, doing work important to the welfare of the group.

The group, starting from the unit of the immediate family of birth, but expanding through systematic introduction into wider areas until it includes eventually the entire universe, is the focus to which the behavior and feeling and entire being of an individual is oriented. Much, if not all, of what a person thinks and does, has a reference to the group. For example, if I go visiting a new mother in my society, I shall probably smile with the joy of seeing her again, with congratulations for her new baby. The Hopi visitor will smile, also, but here the smile has a significance beyond this, as the happiness it expresses helps the baby to thrive and the new mother to recover her strength; and, conversely, a face expressing worry would bring harm at this time.

A person enters this unit by birth, and all of an individual's behavior is geared to this social unit which he has joined through no choice of his own. His loyalties are to this group; they are not person-to-person loyalties. And parents have been known deliberately to try to shift a child's affection from concentration upon one family member, to diffusion among the group. The area of an individual's work, of responsible participation, is therefore not one he has chosen, but is a given also, as it is coextensive with the group. Every individual, young and old, is charged with responsibility for the welfare of the social unit; and this they apparently accept voluntarily, considering it good.

Richard Brandt, a philosopher making a study of Hopi ethics, found that his informants considered that one of the main things which make a man ashamed was that of not having any children alive. This "shows sin"; that is, it shows that a man's behavior, his thoughts, his willing, his emotions were not social enough to keep his children alive. People were expected to be ashamed of not helping in cooperative undertakings, not giving, not participating in ceremonials for the welfare of the unit—in this last case the entire universe. No, said the informants, a man need not be ashamed of being poor, or of being dumb, so long as he was good to others.[1] Brandt made arrangements to see informants in absolute secrecy, to protect them against possible criticism; but he found that the informant might not be ready to talk even so until he had made sure that no harm would come to the group from his disclosures.

Related to this is the Hopi reluctance to stand out—to be singled out from the group. Teachers in Hopi schools have reported discomfort and even tears as a reaction to praise in public. It appears that what is in fact disturbing is the comparative evaluation that results in singling out and praising. Hopi do not compare their achievement, nor the importance of their work, and "a highly skilled stone-cutter is perfectly content to accept the same wages as an unskilled day laborer."[2] Children cannot be persuaded to compete in school—in classwork or in playing games. One school reported that the children learned to play basketball easily, and delight in the game; but they cannot be taught to keep score. They play by the hour, without knowing who is winning. The structure of the game, with everyone doing his utmost within his established role, is in a simplified way, similar to the kind of structure we find in the Hopi group.

As I have indicated already, it is not only the physical act, or

[1] Richard B. Brandt, *Hopi Ethics: A Theoretical Analysis*, University of Chicago Press, Chicago, 1954, pp. 42, 71.

[2] Laura Thompson, *Culture in Crisis: A Study of the Hopi Indians*, Harper & Brothers, New York, 1950, p. 94.

overt behavior, which is effective, according to the Hopi view. Thought and will and intent are at least as effective; so that it is not enough for the individual to act peacefully; he must also feel nonaggressive, think harmonious thoughts, and be imbued with a singleness of purpose. It is his duty to be happy, for the sake of the group—a mind in conflict and full of anxiety brings disruption, ill-being, to the social unit, and, at a time of prayer and ceremonial, to the entire universe.

Brandt [3] found that one of the personal traits highly valued was that of being "happy in his heart." One informant told him, "This is like a flower or a cornfield: when in bloom it beautifies the whole earth. . . . It is a kind of gratitude. . . . When you go into the fields you should sing to the corn." Another informant praised a man who, even when upset, made "himself happy while talking" with others. Superficially, this is similar to valued behavior in our own society, too; but with the Hopi, it is an aspect of working for the group.

Human society is a part of a larger structured whole, so an individual cooperates with even more than the members of his human group. Every aspect of nature, plants and rocks and animals, colors and cardinal directions and numbers and sex distinctions, the dead and the living, all have a cooperative share in the maintenance of the universal order. Eventually, the effort of each individual, human or not, goes into this huge whole. And here, too, it is every aspect of a person which counts. The entire being of the Hopi individual affects the balance of nature; and as each individual develops his inner potential, as he enhances his participation, so does the entire universe become invigorated. Not his behavior alone, not his achievement, but his entire unique being is significant.

Much of the time and energy of the Hopi goes into working at ceremonials. These are highly organized and form part of an established ceremonial cycle. Each ceremony "belongs to" a secret society, usually a man's society and only members of this society have the privilege and the responsibility to carry out the ceremony. Each main ceremony involves an exceedingly complex order of detailed acts: preparatory rites, acts of purification, gathering of

[3] Brandt, *op. cit.*, p. 128.

materials, preparation of masks, sand paintings, and medicine water; composition of new songs, rehearsal of dances. The women prepare food to be exchanged reciprocally. The ceremonials themselves last nine or seventeen days. Though only one secret society is charged with the responsibility of a specific ceremony, the entire group of "spectators"—all the villagers and visitors from other pueblos who come to the public performances—eventually participate, through keeping a "good heart," through their wholehearted involvement in what they watch, through laughing at the burlesque and pranks afforded by the clowns.

Each main ceremony has reference to a phase of the agricultural cycle, helping the universal order to become actual. There is an established course for the sun, for example, within the cosmic order; but the winter solstice ceremony is necessary to actualize this order into the here and now, so that the sun can actually follow the prescribed course, and so turn northward. The growing of the corn also has its established order; the stages of growth are given in the order of nature; but the corn cannot move through them, from germination to fruition, without the cooperative effort of man, who must transform, by means of his ceremonials, potentiality into actuality. So, in the end, when a field of corn is ready to harvest, it is a result of the cooperative effort of every member of the group, in addition to the man who has dug and hoed and planted and weeded.

Though each ceremonial has specific reference within the agricultural cycle, each main ceremony also has reference to the whole of life, to the entire cosmic system. The aim is the well-being of the universal whole, not of the individual. If the individual profits by the ceremonial, it is because he is an integral part of this whole which has become invigorated. The individual maintains harmony with the universe for the sake of the universal order, not for his own sake, except derivatively. Eventually, through the maintenance of this harmony, the human group thrives, the sun moves along its established course from solstice to solstice, the thunderclouds gather and release their rain, the corn sprouts and roots and fills and ripens.

In all this, the individual is working along given lines, for given ends, for a group which he did not create of his own choice. This seems the denial of all freedom and initiative.

In addition, the geographic location of the Hopi seems to make for determinism, and an absence of individual freedom. They live and practice agriculture in country where it would seem, offhand, to be impossible to depend on the land for a living. The rain may not come at all, or may fall in torrents and wash away the crops; high winds may blow away the seed. The growing cycle of corn, their main crop, is almost coincidental with the growing season, which is cut short at both ends by killing frosts. As Laura Thompson says: "The arid north Arizona plateau posed unyielding imperatives which had to be met habitually and unerringly if the tribe were to survive and reproduce itself. . . ."[4] This means that the environment imposes rigid limits to behavior and choice. How can man have personal freedom, if these circumstances, to will, to act, to be, when the very environment dictates behavior, and where there is so little margin for human fallibility? Where can there be room for personal initiative? Who can be proud of his stand of corn when even the laughter of a child has gone to grow it? How can there be motivation for work, when the responsibility, and the results and the work itself are all shared, to a greater or less extent? Does not this mean that personal effort is lost in the undifferentiated immensity, that the individual is submerged and lost in the group and the universe?

Strange to say, the genius of the Hopi culture has made it possible to find spontaneity, significance and freedom, motivation and personal integrity, within this structured universe, within the given society, and the difficult environment. It is true that there is probably no joy of independent achievement, but this does not mean that there is no motivation, no personal initiative.

Certainly, there is no such thing as individualism, in our sense of the term. There is no private enterprise, no joy of personal success; and there is avoidance of outstandingness. There is no undertaking which an individual initiates and brings to a conclusion alone, with

[4] Thompson, *op. cit.*, pp. 173–174.

the pride of success. When a farmer is harvesting a "successful" corn crop, who had "succeeded"? Throughout the year, the members of his pueblo, in different organizations, have performed successive ceremonies, to bring about this harvest. The children have played organized ball games for days with the children from another pueblo, and thus helped the corn to grow. Men have refrained from intercourse with their wives, and sweethearts; eaglets have been captured at considerable risk, women and children have laughed heartily at the antics of ceremonial clowns, priests have gone into retirement and meditation, and much more has been done and wished and thought, to bring about this good harvest. The farmer's achievement in all this may be seen as insignificant; yet it may also be seen as superbly significant.

For the immensity of effort is not undifferentiated; the individual effort is not like a grain of sand, lost in the universal whole. Every individual within the system has his unique role, and each role is different and indispensable. The structured whole of the universe, or of the human group, contains a precise position for each and every member. No one is expendable. "Every individual in the group, male and female, young or old, has his proper place and role in the organization of the community, with corresponding duties and privileges . . . with duties and rights commensurate with their age and status." [5] And, in the universal whole, every part of nature has its unique and indispensable role. Man supplies the moving principle in this order through his ability to will, and through his ceremonials.

So man, each individual person, through the uniqueness of his role, and the indispensability of his own specific effort, has great significance. Group effort and community of ends, does not mean totalitarianism and the loss of individual uniqueness. In fact, the group can prosper only in so far as this uniqueness is fully actualized. Only in so far as each member of each *kiva* carries out his own unique responsibility, fulfils his role in putting on and performing the ceremony which is the responsibility of this particular ceremonial association, will the ceremony help the corn to move into the next

[5] *Ibid.*, p. 65.

stage of growth. In this each individual member has an indispensable and precise function.

The clarity of role, the preciseness of structure and of place in the structure is such that the individual knows what is open to him to do; and, as it is apparently satisfying to work in terms of the social unit, the individual can and does work autonomously within his role. O'Kane writes, "A Hopi household is a self-directing group, the members of which seem to achieve automatic coordination of their activities. No one tells the others what they should do, or when, or how. No one exercises authority. The various members seem to fall naturally into a pattern in which the abilities of the individual and the needs of the household are satisfactorily served . . ." [6]

Thus an individual can decide to what extent he will fill the responsibility which is his privilege. For example, O'Kane tells how three fellow clansmen decided to get turtles to supply themselves with shell for the leg rattles used in ceremonial dancing. This was done at their own initiative, but within an established framework—*i.e.*, the rattles were to be attached to a specified part of the leg, they were to be of specified shell, worn at specified times in specified roles, etc. The individual decision brought more shell rattles, or newer rattles to the *kivas* involved; it enriched the group. The decision involved much and arduous work, including a return journey of some six hundred miles. Each of the three contributed of what he had to offer—one his car, another gas, the third his knowledge and skill. There was no attempt at uniformity, nor at equalization; there was no suppression of individuality; rather through the variety of individual contribution, the whole could be achieved.

The individual is free to choose ways in which to actualize his responsibility; as, for example, when three children asked to stay after school because their grandmother was dying in their home, as they were afraid that they could not avoid anxious thoughts if they went back to the pueblo. Responsible group participation is felt as a happy occasion, as projective tests given to Hopi children

    [6] Walter Collins O'Kane, *The Hopis: Portrait of a Desert People,* University of Oklahoma, Norman, 1953, p. 8.

show. And a marked correlation exists between the presence of spontaneity in the personality, as revealed in the tests, and degree of participation in the communal life of the pueblo.

It is clear that the welfare of the group and of the entire universe eventually depends on the individual; yet the individual is not tethered, nor monitored, nor shackled, nor coerced, to insure his safe carrying out of his responsibilities. When Brandt was asking questions involving ethical principles, he found that there was no adherence to group morals as categorical. "It is up to him to decide" what is right or wrong, was stated repeatedly, as well as the desirability of consent: "I don't believe in forcing anybody to do anything. . . . If he gives his consent, it is all right." [7]

It is evident, then, that a tremendous respect and trust is accorded to the individual since no provision is made for man's failure, neglect, error. The entire group and the entire universe is vulnerable, exposed to the fallibility of the individual. Even a child, allowing himself to have anxious thoughts, can bring ill to the pueblo. This means a great responsibility, and can be seen as a frightening and overwhelming burden. Yet, instead of blocking the individual with its immensity, this responsibility seems to function as a motivating factor, affording a channel for spontaneity. Instead of cutting off the protruding variations, the peculiar differentiating qualities of the individual; instead of submerging the self within a uniform mass, the group encourages individual quality, and enriches itself through it. The significant place given to each unique person and the full trust accorded to each, means that the group can thrive through the full exercise of the individual self.

This is what I had missed in the school situation of my children; I had missed significance and respect for unique being. There was no trust in the potentiality of each child. The homeroom protected itself against its members; it would not take a chance on the honesty or mathematical ability or industry of its members. The individual had no significance; and, in fact, all effort was made to make the members of the group interchangeable, until the artistic expression of one could not be distinguished from that of another. There was

[7] Brandt, *op. cit.*, pp. 190, 191, 203, 221, 224, 225, 229.

no appreciation of individual quality; it was treated as disruptive and threatening of group welfare, and, being cast into the outer darkness, it did, in fact, disrupt. If my son could have drawn the Egyptian war scene in his own peculiar lines, he would have had no occasion to introduce his minute discordant bird in the corner. Some growth of the self did occur, because of its tremendous impetus; but it met with discouragement. I found here that the group existed at the expense of the individual; and this was totalitarianism.

At this point my problem was clear and I solved it. What did I do? I decided that I needed a school where the group was conceived according to democratic principles: where the individual was given a significant place within the structured group; where the group was considered to prosper only through the optimum growth of each and every member—not through stunting them; where uniqueness was valued; where individual and group could grow and thrive only together. I found such a school and moved to the town where it was, forty miles away. I solved my problem. My children are growing up in true American democracy.

BIBLIOGRAPHY

(References have been made only to those items
from which direct quotations were given)

Richard B. Brandt, *Hopi Ethics: A Theoretical Analysis,* University of Chicago Press, Chicago, 1954.

Walter Collins O'Kane, *The Hopis: Portrait of a Desert People,* University of Oklahoma, Norman, 1953.

Leo W. Simmons, *Sun Chief: The Autobiography of a Hopi Indian,* Yale University Press, New Haven, 1942.

Alexander M. Stephen, *Hopi Journal,* edited by Elsie Clews Parsons, Columbia University Press, New York, 1936.

Laura Thompson, *Culture in Crisis: A Study of the Hopi Indians,* Harper & Brothers, New York, 1950.

Laura Thompson and Alice Joseph, *The Hopi Way,* University of Chicago Press, Chicago, 1944.

IX

THE ARTIST AND HIS SOCIETY

BY

GEORGE L. K. MORRIS

The position in which the painter or sculptor finds himself today is—as far as I know—something unique in history. We could doubtless extend much of what I am saying to include the poet and the composer as well. At any rate, the so-called "esthetically-creative" professions are nowadays beset with contradictions and dilemmas all their own. On the one hand, they've never been so susceptible to compromises; at the same time they offer unparalleled opportunities for freedom.

Before discussing specifically the various problems of artists, I must narrow my field; I want to make a few qualifications. Perhaps it's superfluous to point out that within modern society—albeit somewhat pushed around the fringes—painters and sculptors seem to fall into quite divergent categories. To be sure any classification of artists is apt to be hazardous. And I want it understood that I'm dividing them here—not according to the scope of their work—but in relation to society with which they must connect.

Most familiar to the public are the so-called "commercial-artists." These are the ones who illustrate the *Saturday Evening Post,* who paint for reproduction in butchers' calendars, who execute the advertisements we meet everywhere, from the pages of periodicals to the subway. Such illustrators are geared to a public that is not expected to look for very long; it usually sees the work only in reproduction. Yet it is the commercial artists who constitute what great masses of the public think of as A R T—in such moments, that is, as the subject reaches them at all. There are degrees of quality here, of course. But I think it can be said that the real emphasis is

93

on salesmanship. Their problems are more closely allied to that of the businessman; they don't come within our province here at all.

We now arrive at a second category; this one also depends for its existence on an ability to satisfy a public. It is more sophisticated, perhaps, but hardly more elevated in taste. I should include here the fabricators of our public monuments. (They are usually required to ingratiate some board of civic councillors, whose eyes have been nurtured on the standards of category one.) There are also the society portrait-painters and official illustrators (who must concentrate on a flattering replica that will enhance the client's community-standing—no place here for values that are the prerequisites of art), the decorators of public buildings, banks, and—saddest of all—religious and educational edifices. (Here again the client is apt to be a board of trustees, who think chiefly of maintaining their position.)

Now why should there be anything wrong in trying to please one's patrons?—you may well ask in art as in anything else. They succeeded in doing just that during most great periods of the past; if that answer were still valid today I could stop right here with my first two categories, instead of merely passing them by in an introduction. When those in power are individuals of taste and discernment—however reprehensible they may be in other respects—great things can be accomplished. So it was that during the Renaissance artists worked for clients whom they surely aimed to please, and the results have been a wonder to the world ever since. Why is it that Art—the art that is shown in museums, that is now taken seriously by intelligent people everywhere—has in modern times been taking forms that seem incomprehensible and even a joke to the public? The artist doesn't enjoy his new position, certainly; he has to suffer for it most of all.

I have time here only to trace the progression somewhat sketchily. It was during the past century that an unprecedented situation arose. A new civilization began to emerge—based on industrialization, mechanization, and widely diversified sources of wealth. People found so many new things to occupy them that they didn't seem to require art any more. Not certainly as a natural background for their daily lives. An occasional glance at superficial works in an exhibition, or on a building as one hurried by—that was enough. Something time-tested and safe was all right to have around—there was a little time still for Old Masters, the mark of a counterfeit aristocracy that was no longer there. They would tolerate new works, too, that bore a casual resemblance to what their eyes had been trained to accept. And it wasn't long before the most trifling illustrations sufficed. Man, with his new-found knowledge of the physical universe, began to feel he could get along without spiritual nourishment. The new and all-important "leisure-classes" felt that they could settle for more cheerful and less exigent ways of wasting time.

Is it in any way strange that, in such an atmosphere, the taste of enlightened patronage collapsed? Through all this, artists of integrity were becoming uneasy. A few of them began to take matters into their own hands. They rebelled at devoting their lives to such stale canvases and marbles as they encountered in the official academies and salons. They aimed rather—in the words of Cézanne—to produce an art "that would be solid, like the art of the museums." Furthermore, an art must emerge which would have a fresh *look* about it, appropriate to the new civilization they were just beginning to know. It had to be done regardless of what any one thought. And so we have the countless art-movements—impressionism, cubism, futurism, abstraction—that lead up to the art of today. Not everything was a success, but at least character and integrity began to reappear. And each new movement, and the life of almost every artist who contributed, was a tale of poverty, bitterness, and frustration. To be sure—years after each new direction had reached its prime—small sections of the public would catch up. And we see the crowds who now pour into the Van Gogh exhibitions; it is said that post-Impressionist reproductions have displaced Maxfield Parrish on the walls of student dormitories; and I understand that at the moment [December, 1955] people stand out on Fifth Avenue, awaiting their turn to get into the Guggenheim Museum for a glimpse of the fabulous sculpture of Brancusi.

I'm now in a position—with a certain understanding between us, I hope—for some analysis. You have probably guessed that I am bringing forward my third category of artists. Certainly these are not commercial artists; they'd be flops in commerce of any kind. Nor do they produce paintings or sculptures aimed primarily at making money—though they are very glad to take in anything they can get, of course. No one in his right mind would embark on such a career in America today if his chief aim were to secure material rewards. Certainly there must be something else, in this third category, known in the local patois as "serious artists." Perhaps a better term was contributed by the late Mayor Hylan, when he once referred to them as *Art-artists* ("I don't like Art-artists"). Do they have a common denominator? Only that they are gnawed at by something within, for the expression of which they will forego security, stability, and even the comforts of life. There is a force inside them for which they *must* find release; they want to deliver it in a tangible form that will communicate itself to others; they want to hang it up, this authentic fragment of themselves, to have posterity keep on connecting with it behind the safety of museum walls. A poor substitute, this, for the walls of buildings people use! It's a mixture of all kinds of impulses, glorified and base. There is egotism, exhibitionism, false aggrandizement of self, snobbism, that desire we used to talk about in our adolescent days—*"épater les bourgeois."* And somewhere beneath these divergent currents of self, perhaps a heroic impulse that will follow the problem of deliverance to the end. At this stage the artist takes a position not so different from that of the preacher or the prophet—some force on fire within that can admit no compromise.

I remember the sculptor Lachaise, when he once remarked with fervor, "All art is a confession!" What he meant was that in an artist's work everything is sure to come out—his personality, his strength, his integrity. So it is that those who are sensitive can feel so violently about works of art. For they are fragments of life itself. Before the dilemmas of life today no wonder that only the hardiest talents can survive. A sign of weakness, we will find, and anxiety, always stalking in the background, ready to overwhelm its prey.

Here is our third category, and when I use the word "artist" from now on, it is to this ill-assorted company that I shall be referring. It's time now to look a little more closely at this strange struggle for survival, and you will understand reasons for the essential compromises. I don't know how many "Art-artists" there are—the number must be up in the thousands, with countless students in addition already steeling themselves for the ordeal. Even the public begins to be curious about their work, which fairly bursts the walls of our local and national museum-shows, not to mention a hundred-odd New York galleries. That their primary purpose is not the making of money proves to be an understatement. You would be astonished if I told you how few make a living exclusively from the sale of their own paintings or sculptures. Out of thousands you could count them on your fingers with a few to spare.

Perhaps you are not familiar with the method by which an artist sells his wares in this devious world of ours. If he is to have any protracted connection with a public now-a-days, he must become affiliated with a dealer, who is usually located in New York. This is not easy; when it is accomplished the dealer, every few years, puts on a show of his work (in many galleries the artist has to pay for this privilege); in addition, the dealer keeps samples always on hand to show clients who drop by; if he is lucky enough to make a sale he is rewarded by a forty percent commission. And then there are the museum-directors who amble in, to pick up wares for the "Annuals," as they're called. There is the possibility of a prize—but usually the artist loses contact with his work sometimes for a year or two on a museum-circuit. Many people may see it, but all the artist gets is nicked frames or chips off his sculpture-bases. The plastic arts have a different relation to their audiences than have literature and music. Any one who buys a work of art must buy the actual object. Others may find it interesting, or even love it, yet without the available purchase-price, the artist receives no tangible benefit. And of the few who can buy, a majority prefer the glamor of some foreign artist, with his unusual name and picturesque overtones.

I shan't go on indefinitely sounding the woes of the American painter and sculptor. You might be surprised to find perhaps that they constitute the most cheerful segment of contemporary society;

they have a sense of accomplishment in a field that they love; also a hope for the future that is not based on material success, a conception that so many of their compatriots have lost. My purpose is merely to emphasize that they turn elsewhere if they are to find a living wage.

Has there ever been such a dilemma? Those who are engaged in shaping the culture of our time—by whom, we have been told by historians, we shall be known to posterity—are not able to eke out even a minimum existence from the fruits of toil, for which they would gladly give their lives. They must turn over much priceless time and energy to some more lucrative form of occupation, usually they must do it in some clearcut line of duty. For whatever may be the scope of an artist's hopes and passions he must still exist as a human being in the contemporary world. He must fulfil certain personal obligations like every one else. He has a duty to his family, duty to his minimum personal needs. The act of bringing these about we might call the "honest compromises." It enables the artist to live, and to continue his chosen path during whatever hours of the day or night are left over to him. Even in his daily social contacts how is he to comport himself? In other professions—lawyers, doctors, businessmen—there seem to be common bases of contact. But the artist is apart—people he meets seem to have nothing to say that has much real meaning for him. I know it myself so well —how often I will pick up acquaintance with a stranger; we will seem to be getting on amicably enough; and then he asks, "What is your business?" I answer that I am an artist. Still hopefully he wants to know what kind. For a moment I would give anything to say truthfully that I was working on a portrait of Mrs. Roosevelt, or an ad for Lucky Strike. But the facts must come out—I am an abstract painter, and the conversation palls behind an insuperable barrier.

How should an artist fit into his community—particularly on an income that the average broker's secretary would consider inappropriate to her station? Frequently he has a family that would like ordinary contacts. They have to adjust as best they can; he goes about in semi-solitude, coming to life only in the presence of his fellow-artists or that occasional person who "seems to understand." How should he assume the usual responsibilities of citizenship? It is not by coincidence that artists have been perhaps the easiest prey to political doctrines that give promise of social upheaval —ever since Courbet headed a group of painters who pulled down the column in the Place Vendome. In France, moreover, artists, I am told, are automatically barred from jury duty, as it is presumed they are anarchists. And in time of war should they give up fleeting years, in which they could conceivably render more glory to their country than as mediocre foot-soldiers? Which direction here would be considered a compromise? There is more to it than one artist —who, let us hope, was apocryphal—has answered it, "You are all fighting for the culture that I represent."

But we must return to these legitimate compromises that keep body and soul together. Art-teaching is thought of as the most "congenial," with the added advantage of being usually limited to only two or three days a week. However, except in the case of a well-organized personality, teaching is not as congenial as one might think. I know, because I've tried it. The creative act—almost like a mystical experience—is something highly sensitive and internal. To talk about it to others may drain it of its essential spontaneity. So it is that many artists rely on jobs as removed as possible from the path of art. I know many who have held down every sort of occupation, from boiler-mender to tug-boat captain on the East River; anything that will tide them over until a little capital can be accumulated for a fulltime return to their rightful professions. In the meantime they may be classed as Sunday-painters or amateurs, but at least their art has not been debased. I have certain friends who evolved an ingenious compromise of a sort. They secured jobs as guards at the Metropolitan Museum. They would study the paintings by day, then go home and paint in the evening. As guards they may not have been very alert, however.

I know many artists who have fallen into a deeper compromise. There have been many endowed with astonishing facility in drawing and painting; they have felt that it could all be made use of toward lucrative ends, until their more deeply felt expression could make them self-supporting. They would change just for the time being, and move over into our old categories one and two. They had a genuine contempt for commerical art and society portraiture, but they would practice it tongue-in-check. In debasing their sense of quality, they had forgotten that "Art is a Confession." For an artist to degrade what is most sacred to him is a sin indeed. The release again of forces that depend on nobility and truth requires a long period of expiation. Such artists have paid heavily, and most of them have remained in the paths where they chose to stray.

Yet no one can be too critical of compromises forced by necessity. Unless an artist has independent means or the temporary succor provided by a Fulbright or a Guggenheim, no one can suggest much of an alternative. I have indicated at some length that it is the dream of every serious artist in America that sooner or later the time will come when his creative work will give him adequate security. Esthetic conceptions have been forming in his mind, certain principles upon which his work is based. He has been exerting himself to the utmost and is ready for the one-man show. The essential ads are in the periodicals (the critics aren't apt to come if they are not), and invitations are in the mail. The artist is understandably keyed up as he sees the results of several years' hopes and dreams beginning to ornament the walls. He forgets for a moment that he is in competition for news-space and public attention with scores of other openings. How inevitable the let-down; after friends have strolled away on the opening afternoon, the attendance seems to dwindle to a trickle; and at the week-end, where are the understanding reviews that had been imagined? only a skimpy paragraph thumped out by some impudent nobody.

It requires a supremely inflexible character to stand up after a few rounds of such treatment. Most ordinary mortals would begin to realize that there may have been something they had missed in the American publicity-system. They will see what it means to catch the eye of a museum director, for instance. They soon notice what the art page layouts seem to favor. They will inflate paintings to five times their content in order to be hung in the center at a national show. They see what is quality compared to the aggrandize-

ment of the sacred ego; that such and such a type of work is suddenly beginning to sell. Shouldn't an artist be aware that he can
force his expressive impact to entice new clients? He might have
done better in the end to have taken Brancusi as his model. Brancusi,
who never made an effort to sell his work, has not even had an
exhibition in Paris, although it has long been his home. Instead
of the usual social contacts, his spare time was devoted to the reading of Hindu philosophy. Now alone and old and not able to work
any more he can look at his work and realize that there has been
no compromise.

I have never maintained that an artist should categorically object
to pleasing every one—if he can do so with his integrity intact.
Where would the greatest monuments in art history be, if their
creators had failed to please the Pharaohs, the Medicis, the arrogant
kings of Spain? I can only reiterate that in those days human existence was carried along on a different basis. How restricted seems
the very presentation of art today—the gallery where the artist puts
up his work, and the small personal effusion that he must struggle
with in solitude! This terrible emphasis on self: how easily has it
led the artists of today into a sort of mass-megalomania! To himself
he is ridiculously aggrandized. To society he is nothing at all. A
great contrast from Titian, let us say, who was painting Charles V
with every desire to please his patron. And when he dropped his
brush the emperor picked it up with the words, "It is fitting for
Caesar to pick up the brush of Titian."

During the periods which I've been offering as a contrast, the
spirit fostered by the great religions brought something into art
that we no longer find there. For it was religion that began the
nurture of art, in the most ancient eras. In all periods, religion has
provided the ideal outlet for artistic expression; it kept the creator's
ego subservient to his aim. Something noble and exalted was offered
that was just outside the artist's reach; yet he could express it—
and in very personal and appropriate terms—because it was very
real to him, regardless of the character of his faith. The patron himself may have been a dubious personality by any moral standard.
But he must also keep himself in abeyance if he were to retain

his position. Moreover, he understood the power of art to intensify
the living beliefs of a people; also to advertise his own accomplishments and all that he stood for. So it was that from the glittering
mosaics of Ravenna to the operatic grandeur of Tiepolo, the Italian
world carried through in intimate connection with all-pervading
forces beyond material being. We can find the same thing in every
faith, as far as those overpowering monoliths that glower from
hillsides of Easter Island. And now it has all been frittered away
before the arrogance of man, who has become so wonderful that
he has no more time to be wise.

This has been the real compromise, that rewards us with ugliness
on every side. In the bustle of this modern world, that seems to provide everything for everyone as it marches them to destruction, how
can an artist buck the very forces he must use for his expression?
Who can recover the unrelenting line that with such sureness bound
Fra Angelico to God, as he worked in his little monastery cell?

The tale has been one of progressive diffusion. Gradually the
artist has imbibed the arrogance of his time; he has substituted himself for the forces of religion. It has been quite mutual; the religious
denominations, in turn, have found no place for the great third
category, the serious artists who are fated to deliver the spirit of
their era. Perhaps it will not always be like this. There are signs
that certain enlightened dignitaries are growing conscious that important art can indeed become a driving force in company with
religion; that they can be joined to the incalculable advantage of
each.

A leading British sculptor and painter were recently commissioned to decorate a Protestant church in England. Unhappily there
was a compromise; perhaps it was felt that a genuine expression
would be too much for the parishioners. At any rate, the results
proved quite different from the characteristic work of the two artists,
with a dangerous aberration toward category two. But it may lead
to something more significant at another time. Two or three syna-
gogues in America have commissioned modern painters and sculptors
to execute decorations. These are on a small scale, but at least it is a

beginning. And in France the Catholic Church can count the most notable attempts at integration that we can find in recent years. Most important is undoubtedly the Matisse chapel in Vence, on the Riviera. After the War, Matisse was nursed back to health—after a serious operation—by the nuns of a small convent. He offered to decorate a chapel for them, in gratitude for what seemed a miracle. Although over eighty and forced by his illness to execute most of his designs from a reclining position, he nevertheless succeeded in his contribution. And the result is probably the first outstanding work for a religious edifice since Delacroix painted his frescoes in Saint Sulpice, a hundred years before. A hundred years—that's a long time for a separation between religion and great art.

Four years ago Matisse made the formal presentation of the building with a letter to the Bishop of Nice. It had been entirely his creation—murals for the walls, stained glass for the windows, furniture, doors, even the vestments for the priests and nuns. The Bishop spoke very movingly:

The human author of all that we see here is a man of genius who, all his life, worked, searched, strained himself, in a long and bitter struggle, to draw near the truth and the light . . .

Remember the parable, "it is not he who conceals the talents granted him by God, so as to guard them selfishly, who deserves to be rewarded, but he who at the price of much labor and suffering, having made the talents he received bear fruit, returns them to God on the day of accounting. Then truly he deserves to be called: good and loyal servant."

The private beliefs of Matisse, and his relation to the Church are a bit obscure. But a few years ago he wrote revealingly in a magazine article:

WHETHER I BELIEVE IN GOD? Yes, when I work. When I am submissive and modest, I feel somehow aided by Someone who makes me do things which are beyond me. However, I do not feel towards Him any obligation because it is as if I were before a magician whose tricks I cannot see through. Consequently I feel deprived of the experience which ought to have been the reward of my own effort. I am ungrateful without remorse.

Perhaps it is not the nature of the artist's belief that is all-important. We have no way of knowing how skeptical some of the great artists of the past may have been. The crucial point is the orientation, and that art and religion are the two forces for good in the world today that support each other and can again be brought to a point of fusion. For in the modern world, with the emphasis so strongly on the destruction of men's souls, we have here kindred forces. They can give a measure of stability to the human spirit if they can pursue a path together without compromise.

X

WHAT IS THE RIGHT THING?

BY

EUGENE EXMAN

At the outset it is well to consider that dilemmas are not of themselves undesirable. Dilemmas are like rocks and weeds in a garden; we cope with them in an effort to create a few square yards of landscaped beauty. They are like the resisting water against which a swimmer contends to gain strength. By contending with the elements of choice, presented by dilemmas, we have a sure means of moral growth. To live is to make choices between right or wrong, between greater and lesser good, and each day presents its quota, whether one is selling apples on a street corner or directing the country's largest business corporation.

It does not follow, however, that in any given situation we may be sure what is the right and what is the wrong choice. None of us is sufficiently wise always to know what the right choice is. Furthermore, it is obviously true that what is valid for one person in a specific time and society is not a criterion for another person in a differing period or culture. Nevertheless, we may not hide behind a syllogism set up to prove the impossibility of ever making perfect choices. It is enough to recognize the limitations of our knowledge and experience and the relativity of ethical action. The issue is, in fact, not how to live in a world free of compromise, but how in the dilemmas of an imperfect world to choose what is in the direction of perfection.

When Ivan Ilyich, the successful judge created by Tolstoy, lies dying, he relives the experiences of his years. At first he can see nothing wrong with his life, the motto of which has been to "live pleasantly." But just before the end, a clear insight into his real being comes to him. "Everything," he tells himself, "which you lived is a lie, a deception which conceals you from life and death. . . . What is the right thing?" Thus Tolstoy phrases one of our main dilemmas. "What is the right thing?"

According to Immanuel Kant, man has by nature an altogether inward compulsion to right conduct. Kant's categorical imperative relates ethical behavior to this inner sense of compulsive duty. "Act in such a way," he once wrote, "that you use human nature both in your own person and in everyone else's always as an end, and never as a means." Albert Schweitzer, who was much influenced by Kant, would broaden this criterion to all that lives and his "imperative," "reverence for life," includes what the late Dean W. R. Inge once called "our cousins of fur and feathers."

But even though we drive along a road well marked for ethical action, we often fail to make the right turns. Personal habits obscure our vision. Social customs sometimes block the road. And through lack of will we often take what seems to be an easier, quicker way. Although a road map helps, our dilemma remains: What is the right thing?

Doing the right thing in the world of business is in part conditioned by choice of vocation. If a man finds himself in a job that causes him mental, spiritual, or physical anguish, he faces one of life's most distressing dilemmas. I know a man who gave up a lucrative job in an advertising agency because he came increasingly to believe that most of the time he was writing copy to encourage people to buy products that were not good for them and were, in fact, often harmful. When last I heard he was doing free-lance work, getting an occasional account whose products he considered socially desirable. Thus he effected a compromise, sacrificing income and the security of regular office work. Others sensitive to this problem have made different compromises, from the extreme of turning to other employment to that of rationalizing their work on the ground of expediency. If they turned to other employment they sought what Buddha put fifth in his Eightfold Path, right livelihood. If they compromised their dilemma by staying, they argued that they were expert craftsmen; under the necessity of earning a living they did what was required; if some unwisely bought products through the stimulus of their work, the responsibility involved was social not personal.

For religious persons the dilemma of the right vocation is more acute than ordinarily because they see the compromises that they and others make in relation to a perfection that is more than human. The religious experience, as Reinhold Niebuhr has observed, tends to intensify our belief both in divine truth and righteousness, and in human frailty and sinfulness. The command, "Be ye also perfect," makes the dilemma of choice all the more serious and less likely of easy compromise. When religious insight becomes formalized into creedal sanctions, however, our dilemmas tend to become divorced from moral choice. When we act according to custom rather than to vision, we tend to lose the virtue implicit in ethical choice, and as T. S. Eliot puts it,

> The last temptation is the greatest treason:
> To do the right deed for the wrong reason.[1]

Therefore action must always be subpoenaed to come before the court of the mind. Similarly, intuitional insight must be judged by rational analysis. Religion should never be divorced from reason.

Religious insight and intellectual discrimination are not, however, the only factors that determine the explosive quality of a vocational dilemma. Bodily physique is also a determining factor of greater significance than most persons allow. In his laboratories of Constitutional Psychology, Dr. William H. Sheldon and his associates have photographed and studied more than eighty thousand men and women. These he divides into 88 somatotypes, or examples of physical variation. Sheldon shows a correlation of physique and temperament. Thus a man high in endomorphy, that is a fat man—not a muscular man or a tall, thin man—can accommodate himself most easily to work that is ethically, physically, or esthetically undesirable. For him the dilemma threshold is low and he moves easily into situations that would surely spawn vocational dilemmas for the meso-

---

[1] *Murder in the Cathedral*, Harcourt, Brace & Company, New York, 1935, page 44.

morph or ectomorph. Obviously I am exaggerating to make my point, but even common sense, as well as Sheldon's somatotype charts, shows that a correlation exists between a man's physique and his vocational adaptability. Moreover, dilemmas exist not only for him who labors but also for him who employs labor. A man I know gives much credit to Sheldon for his success—a business that increases in volume at the rate of a million dollars a year. He says he now knows what somatotypes make the best engineers, the best salesmen, the best bookkeepers, etc. All who engage the services of others would face fewer dilemmas and compromises when adding to their staffs if they gave some consideration to somatotypes.

Doing the right thing in business involves much more than choosing the right job or compromising a vocational ideal. The kind of business world we live in affects and often controls action. Dilemmas exist for those who enjoy their work and make it a means to the good life; their dilemmas arise from the very nature of business and industry. If a strike is called a member of the union must walk out whether he wants to or not. To keep a job a man sometimes must pay a large price in hours and service given. A pacifist must struggle with his conscience if in wartime his factory is ordered to turn plowshares into swords. A conscientious executive must decide whether to reduce salaries, curtail staff, or lower standards of production if otherwise he cannot meet competition or survive in a business recession. The ethics of business is never free of the dilemma of deciding what is the greatest good for the greatest number.

Decisions made by management sometimes create farreaching conflicts for employees. Take the example of an automobile salesman who writes:

I would like some help on a problem. I have been selling cars for many years. . . . The automobile business, especially in this area, has turned into a racket and most of our competition has been taken over by large metropolitan dealers this last year, the result being "packing" prices on new cars, financing, etc.—anything to confuse the buying public. At present I am the only salesman on our force trying to sell at the suggested factory price, with an honest price on the trade-in and no "pack" in interest and insurance. Shall I continue to operate this way or fall in line with the others, fighting fire with fire . . . ?

That kind of fire fighting rarely puts out the blaze. It wins no medals for moral valor, creates no heroes of ethical action. It is hard to make a case for using a wrong means to achieve a right end. Ends and means are one, as has often been pointed out. Big business, by its very nature, squeezes little man, but little man's dilemma is not resolved by burning up the place to get out of the vise.

Thus to the complexities of our highly organized economic order must be credited many of the dilemmas of today's businessmen. Professor Kenneth Boulding wrote recently that the coercive power of the large group and the conflict between the private and the general interest are society's two most difficult problems. To solve these problems is a challenge to our best thinking. What Boulding calls "the continuing dilemma" can only be resolved by "the sharp sword of truth in the prophetic individual, the penetrating moral insight that cuts through the shams and excuses of even the best organized society."

The growth of technological skill and specialization have brought to many workers the dilemma of monotonous jobs which lack personal meaning and have little if any social significance. Professor Douglas Steere has described what happened to a group when their work did not make sense.

A little squad of day-laborers . . . were hired one morning and put to work under a taciturn grounds foreman. He set them to digging holes some three feet deep. When a hole was finished it was inspected and the workman was ordered to fill it up and to come to another point and to dig another hole of the same depth. This went on for most of the morning and finally the foreman noted the group talking in a huddle and then their spokesman came over and said sullenly, "We're gonna queet: you give us our muney. You ain' a gonna make damn fool outa us." The foreman's eyes narrowed and then understanding broke over him and he said quietly, "Can't you see, we're trying to find out where the broken pipe is." "Oh!" said the man, and after a hurried word with the other workers he returned and said, "Where you wanna us to dig next?" When the frame of the meaning of this physical work was absent, it seemed to debase these men, to rob them of their validity, to destroy their spirit; and it finally became intolerable. When, and only when the frame of meaning was supplied, the physical work became a good.[2]

This dilemma of the job that lacks meaning and may be debilitating physically and spiritually has been widely discussed in our time. Professor Robert Calhoun and Dr. Robert S. Michaelsen among others have written extensively and authoritatively on this theme. Michaelsen has said "the worker [in a factory] is not doing *his* work; he is not working on his property and with his tools. . . . Frequently the worker in the industrial enterprise is closely attached to the machine, and he may find himself not only subordinated to production and profit, but to the machine as well." Of course, drudgery, boredom, and frustration may apply at times to any man's work, but this dilemma of uncongenial work is especially characteristic of our highly organized economic society.

While dilemmas arise from vocational choice and are a genuine part of the world of business, they exist most profoundly because of the condition of our society, of humanity itself. Herein the dilemmas and compromises the businessman makes are the same as those of the professional man, the housewife, or the politician. William James once wrote, "There is something basically wrong with where we stand." He meant that our values are not grounded in reality. Perhaps it follows that unless we find a more secure footing we will compromise the future of the human race—one way of getting rid of dilemmas. What is wrong with where we stand? I suggest three things: our materialistic culture, our avoidance of suffering, and our lack of integrity.

Scientific advances have been so rapid that the late Alfred North Whitehead said in 1944 that the techniques of living had changed faster in his lifetime than in the preceding nineteen hundred years. Everything he had learned as scientific truth in his youth had in his lifetime become either obsolete or "profoundly modified." This rapid shift in our knowledge of the outer world has hardly given

[2] *Time to Spare*, Harper & Brothers, New York, 1949, page 99.

us time to understand the forces we have to deal with. Generations to come will be shocked at the casual way governments and their peoples have translated atomic power into inconceivably deadly weapons. We are children in paper houses playing with matches. Given great material power to handle, we lack the knowledge, insight, and experience to control it.

As we lack the maturity to control the power that science has unleashed, so we lack the discernment to see that the material fruits of technology are sometimes indigestible. One can eat too many green apples of speed, for example. Man, not the machine, is at fault, particularly when the machine and its material goods are made the chief end of man, his goal and that for which he slaves.

We habitually blame materialism on the Communists. They make much use of Dialectical Materialism based on the "dialectical" system of the philosopher Hegel, in which "thesis" is opposed by "antithesis," with a resulting "synthesis." But Hegel must not be blamed for this latter-day materialism. He said he was describing "the laws of the Spirit [which] are the real essence of the universe." In his recent book, *The Dignity of Man,* Russell Davenport brilliantly analyzed the materialistic basis of Communism; then he deftly fitted the shoe on our Western foot. "The thinkers of the free world," he wrote, "believe that the universe was created out of matter by the operation of the laws of matter . . . everything can and must be accounted for in material—naturalistic terms . . . the metascientific view of Marx and Engels is to a great extent the same as that of the Western world."

Against this concept Davenport reaffirmed the spiritual reference, and by "spiritual" he meant "inward-looking consciousness." He died before he could conclude his work, but he was seeking to get Western man off the horns of the materialistic dilemma by probing the mystery and dignity of man's life on earth. He was attempting a fresh philosophical statement of insights and values for which "millions are seeking."

Signs do point to growing concern for spiritual values. Homage paid in our generation to Gandhi and Schweitzer may be a reaction

from materialism. The arts—music, painting, drama—are flourish-
ing. Nonfiction bestsellers as unlike as *Gift from the Sea* and *The
Search for Bridey Murphy* do have this in common: a desire to
search for meaning beyond the usual sensate experiences of our
humdrum lives. The fascination of Helen Keller's life is that she
lives so fully despite her sensory handicaps. We seem to be ready
to move out of the wilderness of materialism but have no Moses
to lead us. Leadership—disinterested leadership—is now our need.
Lack of seership is here our dilemma.

An assumption of our materialistic culture is that we have a right
to comfort and ease and should avoid suffering. But "knowledge
by suffering entereth," wrote Elizabeth Barrett Browning, and the
lives (and deaths) of the world's great often testify to that truth.
Perhaps in seeking comfort and avoiding pain we are getting off
the evolutionary path. Perhaps in avoiding suffering we are shutting
off a source of power. Certainly we should seek to use suffering
creatively when it comes and come it will. Paradoxically, suffering
is most poignantly felt among us at a time when physical comforts
and palliatives to pain are in greatest abundance. Close the door
of the body to suffering and it comes in the window of the mind.
Our dilemma is how, through disciplined living, to come to terms
with our own suffering and by sharing the pain of others to compromise some of the world's tragedy.

Consider the story of Job, one of the oldest stories in our religious
heritage, written out in the form we have it perhaps twenty-five
hundred years ago. Job was successful. He was the leading businessman of his day. And not only had he achieved great fame for his
wealth but also he was acclaimed for his piety and good works. Moreover he was blessed with a loving family and loyal friends and he
served them without thought of repayment or reward. He was
honest, just, and merciful in all his dealings. He did not need to ask,
"What is the right thing?" He knew what was right and he did it.
But he failed. Through accident or theft all his business assets suddenly melted away. His seven sons and three daughters were killed
when a storm wrecked the house in which they were having a
family reunion. Then sickness came to climax his misfortune. Job

became ill with a repulsive disease and his wife in despair told him to "curse God, and die." His three best friends came to rub metaphysical salt into his wounds. They tried to convince him that he had sinned against God, that God was judging him for his wrongs, and that he was running the risk of the greatest of sins by claiming that he was as just as God. But Job disclaimed any such pretension, although admitting that he was saying a few things he thought worthy of putting into print, one of the earliest examples on record of an author in search of a publisher. "Oh that my words were now written! oh that they were printed in a book!"

Thus Job's knowledge of right and wrong did not free him of the dilemma of suffering. In fact, his humility and steadfast faith during his time of suffering is almost unsurpassed, and one of the great affirmations of faith is: "Though He slay me, yet will I trust in Him." Tolstoy also saw the significance of suffering. He has Ivan Ilyich while dying see too late "it was necessary to do something to save them [his family] pain." Instead of seeking to share the burden of suffering carried by others, he had thought only of how "to live pleasantly." To know and to do what is right create dilemmas of a higher kind, dilemmas that may, in fact, be steps of spiritual growth and doorways into sainthood.

Finally, the ground we stand on is unsure because of the widespread lack of integrity. "At no time in the world's history has organized lying been practised so shamelessly or, thanks to modern technology, so efficiently or on so vast a scale as by the political and economic dictators of the present century." So wrote Aldous Huxley in 1937; he would probably say the same today. Expediency is the slogan of the politician. It is the policy of Communism—praising Stalin one day, decrying him the next. Neither integrity nor consistency are virtues and both play second fiddle to expediency. The puzzle, the pathetic paradox, is that the common people of the world around are taken in by dishonesty. Or are they not? Do some see through the screen of propaganda—whether Russian or American or French—and cry out in the silence of their souls for men of integrity? No doubt much of President Eisenhower's popularity is due to the belief people have in his honesty.

As in business, so in political life, so in society at large. In all human relationships the ground of integrity is woefully thin; expediency is the best policy. Or take two other criticisms often leveled at the businessman: his greed for profits and his lust for power. These drives are surely no more characteristic of the businessman than they are of society at large. And these faults, like the basic one of dishonesty, will not be rectified till our whole culture finds a new orientation. No man is guiltless and the lack of integrity, especially, is the sickness of humanity.

"Can the conscious calculated output of untruths, half-truths and misleading irrelevancies," writes a friend, "be continued for a long period without an ever-mounting cost in the currency of character? Can playing fast with truth and sincerity yield peace of mind? It's touching to note how inadequately a man's hard-won cynicism covers the gap between the shirt of respectability and the pants of expediency. I know men to whom the urgency of truth dawned in their middle years, when they were shackled to commercial falsehood by loyalty, by affection, by pride and by habit. Such a man suffers. To regain his soul would cost him his whole world."

Most of the dilemmas of the business world—and their compromises—involve a man's integrity. In the countless choices that comprise the world of buying and selling, the one constant factor should be the integrity of those who meet in the market place. In Arthur Miller's play, *Death of a Salesman,* Willy Loman is depicted as a salesman who at the end of his days makes a futile effort to recapture what is considered his success. The play has been described as a portrayal of the dilemma of modern business which places too great an emphasis on sales. "He's a man way out there in the blue," says Willy's friend, "riding on a smile and a shoeshine . . . Nobody dast blame this man. A salesman is got to dream, boy. It comes with the territory." But the book is not so much an indictment of business, as it is a record of what happens when a man loses his integrity, when he lives a deception. The tragic portrayal of this dilemma and its hapless compromise comes when Willy's son Bif turns from his father, whom he had idolized, crying, "You fake! You phony, little fake." *Death of a Salesman* depicts the dilemma not only of the businessman but of society at large, of everyman: how to safeguard and not to compromise integrity.

Reference was made earlier to the "dialectical" process developed by Hegel. Here we have a clue to handling dilemmas. If the "right thing" be considered a "thesis," then the compromise is the "antithesis" and not the resolution of the conflict. The resolution is a further step; it is the "synthesis." The disparities that exist between what the right thing is (or seems to be) and our compromised action may thus lead to a new synthesis. Perhaps the last half of our century will be an age of synthesis. If so, many of the dilemmas of the businessman, whether inherent in vocation or growing out of the nature of the economic structure or of Western culture itself, may be carried beyond compromises to new solutions. To find this future "synthesis" is an exciting challenge for today.

XI

SOME ISSUES FOR THE LAWYER

BY

HERBERT WECHSLER

When I was asked to speak to you on "Dilemmas and Compromises in the Life of a Jurist," the first thing I did was to consider what a jurist is, because I thought that this was a preliminary question that I had to answer before I knew the role I was to play. On questions such as this, I always turn first to a very helpful volume, the Merriam-Webster Dictionary, and I was interested, somewhat perturbed in fact, to discover that the dictionary definition of a "jurist" lists three meanings:

The first is a "lawyer," but after that there is a little notation, "obsolete." The second is, "one who professes to a knowledge of the law," and although I have been teaching law for almost twenty-five years, I have never reached the point where I could profess to any knowledge of it. The third was "a law student," and I think probably it is in this capacity that I can venture to appear.

But though the jurist as "lawyer" is an obsolete meaning of the term, there are over 200,000 lawyers in the United States and I'm sure that some sense of their problems and the dilemmas and compromises they face would fall within the scope of your inquiry.

Lawyers, after all, are on the whole engaged in three types of occupations: they are counsellors, they are advocates in court—litigators, one might say—and, finally, they are draftsmen of some of the most important secular documents that exist.

On the whole, if we think about their problems, I think it would be fair to say that the deepest and most important would simply parallel all the subjects that have been included in your series. For certainly, as counsellor, what the lawyer does is to share the problems of his clients. As litigator, perhaps he faces special problems, and of these I shall have something to say later. But, on the whole, there well may be the possibility that as litigator, as barrister in the English sense, he faces fewer dilemmas and compromises because his task is clearest in that situation: to present fairly and within the limits of well defined duty the position of his client. As draftsman, I suppose his problems are largely artistic and tactical.

There is another sense, however, in which it may be interesting to think of the jurist, and it is this sense that I shall emphasize, neither that of the counseling, the litigating nor the drafting lawyer, but that of the man of law who is connected in some professional way with the unfolding or the application of law in public affairs.

In the great books it is customary to speak of the lawyer as the legislator and to think of the legislator's problems, or to speak of the lawyer as judge and to think of the judge's problems. This is not the practising professional perspective, the lawyer sharing other people's troubles, attempting to be of help. Rather, this is the sense in which the man of law plays an actual part in the conduct of public affairs by law; and it is at this point, I should say, that the problem of dilemmas and compromises becomes most acute.

The judge always confronts a choice, does he not? Shall he decide one way or the other? The legislator, confronting a much larger number of possibilities, of possible solutions in relation to the affairs of man and of society, at least secular affairs, asks himself: shall I proceed along one course, or along another? Shall I impose one type of norm, or the other type of norm, in the performance of my functions as a lawmaker, or lawgiver?

And so I say that I shall emphasize, in what little I have to say, that function of the jurist in which he plays the role of lawmaker, lawgiver, decider of issues. In choosing to dwell on this phase of juristic life, I think at least that I fall within the pattern of your purpose here, because the important problems of this sort that I have had to face have, on the whole, arisen in the course of public work rather than in the course of private work as a practising attorney.

Of course I should add one other obvious proposition: for every problem, every dilemma, every compromise that must be made in the course of action by a public official, there is, is there not, a reverse and theoretical side of the same issue? When anyone undertakes to function as a critic of what public officials do—all of us as citizens, but jurists especially, in so far as they undertake to function as interpreters or critics of what is done in the name of law—are effective only when they place themselves in the position of the person who had to make the decision, be he the legislator or the judge, and then ask themselves, was this decision right, was it correct, was it the best or the better decision that could have been made? Is it not true that the test of responsible criticism always is, whatever is the subject of criticism, whether the critic has adequately placed himself in the position of the man whose decision he undertakes to criticize.

Sterile criticism is that which fails to make this identification, and so voices either praise or blame divorced from the reality of the situation that is the subject of praise or blame.

You might ask as an initial question, "Why should there be any dilemma or compromise in law? Is not the law clear, ready to be applied equally? Is it not of the nature of law, this clarity?" In this view the jurist has only to know the law, and the course is then clear.

Unfortunately, this is not in the nature of law. Law is not, by nature, clear, precise, discernible. On the contrary, as in any other entity which has its being in words, law is intrinsically uncertain and unclear, a lack of clarity which turns first on the inherent lack of clarity of language, turns secondly on the vagueness of the lawmakers' intention, turns thirdly on the fact that when law is made not all problems and applications are foreseen. It is, in short, of the nature of law that it is shaped as it is applied. Thus all of those who deal with it, even after it has been enacted, face concrete choices of direction; and the discernment of content, which is the act of interpretation is, in part, an act of will.

There is a nice story that I would like to read to you, from a book I very much admire that has just come out and that I commend to you. It's called *The Moral Decision,* and its author is a law professor at New York University, named Edmond Cahn. He takes us to the Babylonian Talmud and, as he tells the story, Rabbi Eliezer is engaged in heated argument with his colleagues over a delicate technical point in the interpretation of the law. Now I'm quoting, of course:

After exhausting all his resources of precedent, distinction, analogy and citation of textual authority without convincing any of them (that is, any of his colleagues) Rabbi Eliezer becomes desperate and cries out, "If the law agrees with me, let this tree prove it." Thereupon, the tree leaps a hundred cubits from its place. Some say 400 cubits. But the other judges calmly retort, "No proof can be adduced from a tree."

Then he says, "If the law agrees with me, let this stream of water prove it." At this the stream of water flows backwards. The others rejoin, however, "No proof can be adduced from a stream of water."

Again he calls out, "If the law agrees with me, let the walls of the house prove it." Whereupon the walls begin to fall. But Rabbi Joshua, one of the sages present, rebukes them, saying, "When scholars are engaged in a legal dispute, what right have you to interfere?", and so they do not fall, out of respect for Rabbi Joshua, nor do they resume the upright, out of respect for Rabbi Eliezer, but remain standing and inclined.

Finally, Rabbi Eliezer says, "If the law agrees with me, let it be proved from Heaven." At that moment a heavenly voice cries out, "Why do you dispute with Rabbi Eliezer, seeing that in all matters the law agrees with him?" For a space the assemblage sits transfixed. But almost immediately Rabbi Joshua rises from his seat and exclaims, "The law is not in Heaven, it was given on Mount Sinai. We pay no attention to a heavenly voice."

Soon thereafter (as the story goes) one of the Rabbis happens to meet the Prophet Elijah who, having been alive when he was transported into the celestial regions, remains able to converse with mortals. The Prophet is asked, "What did the Holy One, blessed be He, do at that point?" The Rabbi replies, "He laughed with joy, saying, 'My sons have defeated me! My sons have defeated me!' " [1]

[1] Edmond Cahn, *The Moral Decision,* Indiana University Press, Bloomington, 1955, pp. 311–312.

This account makes my point, I think. Not all the law was given on Sinai, but that law which is given in the legislature, or given by the courts, has for this purpose the same quality as the law given on Sinai. It's a matter that may be argued about endlessly.

And then, too, there is always an uncertainty as to the facts to which the law is to be applied. Now, if we ask ourselves, "Why is it that the law is thus characteristically uncertain?", surely the answer has been exhibited by the other speakers who have appeared on this series—because law is made for the regulation of life, in society, and life in society is characterized primarily by the multiplicity of values that it presents, from the lowest to the highest.

And so, in the decisions that must be made in law, the real source of the difficulty is in the clash of values, the situation in which it is not possible, with mortal limitations, to realize all the right values to the maximum extent.

This is very abstract, I know. Let me give some illustrations of the kind of thing I mean to say:

To begin with, may I take your minds back some thirteen or fourteen years? I ask you to think of the spring of 1942. The country was at war. The situation—the military and naval situation— was not happy for us.

At this time the Commanding General of the West Coast Command made recommendations to Washington as to his concern about the possible danger to be apprehended from the some hundred thousand persons of Japanese ancestry on the West Coast. Most of these human beings were citizens of the United States, some were aliens, subjects of the Emperor of Japan. However, the alien Japanese group had been subject to internment, under the traditional powers over enemy aliens, and so some 3,000 had been interned.

But the Commanding General's concern went far beyond that, and representations were made to the Department of Justice asking for further protection from this group of people who were feared. One of the authors in this book was then Attorney General of the United States, Mr. Francis Biddle, and I had the honor to be one of his Assistants at that time.

The Department of Justice examined the problem that the military were concerned about. The Federal Bureau of Investigation, a very adept and effective body of law enforcement agents, had substantial knowledge of the West Coast problem.

In the Department of Justice it is a fair statement of the case to say that the view held was that no special security measures were required, that the danger, if there was a danger, could be met by identifying individuals whom there was cause to fear and dealing with them in accordance with law; if they were aliens, by internment; if they were citizens, by arrest in the event they were guilty of violations.

Mr. Biddle presented this position very forcefully to the President of the United States. The contrary position was pressed, however, and pressed very vigorously on the War Department. A great lawyer and a great man was Secretary of War, Henry Stimson. His principal Assistant, in relation to these problems was also, in my view, a great man, Mr. John J. McCloy, who is now the President of the Chase Bank here in New York.

The conferences that were initiated at this point resulted of course in the presentation of these conflicting views as to what were the requirements of military security. In the end it became clear that Secretary of War Stimson, was persuaded that strong action was needed, and this view was presented to the President by Secretary Stimson.

The question that I put to you is, what should have been Mr. Biddle's course at this point, as Attorney General, as the custodian of law in the national administration, the traditional role of any Attorney General? Should he have advised the President of the United States that to undertake the type of action that was called for, namely, really the expulsion of the entire Japanese population, was unconstitutional? Should he have taken that course?

He believed that it was undesirable to take this measure, but that if it were taken the United States Supreme Court would sustain its validity as an extreme war measure.

What he did was to advise the President that the Department of Justice would not take such an action, that if any such action were to be taken, it must be taken by the War Department, and on the responsibility of the military, but that if the military deemed the action to be necessary for the preservation of the country or, as he said, a proper precaution for the defense of the country, that it would probably be sustained by the United States Supreme Court, and on this record and against this background the President of the United States did issue Executive Orders authorizing the Commanding Generals of the various Commands, with the approval of the Secretary of War, to issue orders excluding any individuals or groups from designated areas.

Following the issuance of that order, Congress enacted a statute declaring it to be a civil crime, misdemeanor, for anyone to refuse to obey such an order, and so it was that the entire Japanese population of the West Coast was removed from the West Coast—I should not write "Japanese population," the entire population of persons of Japanese ancestry on the West Coast was removed, and large numbers of the group found themselves in what in any fair estimate should be called "concentration camps," though they were given a more appealing name, they were called "Relocation Centers," and there they stayed for some two years, until the order was finally rescinded.

One of the members of this population, a man by the name of Korematsu, refused to obey the order, and he stood prosecution. The purpose of standing prosecution was to test the constitutionality of the entire program.

It fell to me in my duties as Assistant Attorney General, to superintend the preparation of the brief in support of the constitutionality of the evacuation program, though I think no one could have felt more distressed about its existence, other than those personally affected by it, than I.

Should I have declined to assume the preparation of a brief in support of the constitutionality of what the President of the United States had ordered on the recommendation of his distinguished Secretary of War? I might have done that. In fact, however, I did not. I did superintend the preparation of that brief. It presented the strongest arguments that I felt could be made in support of the validity of the action taken by the President and, in fact, as you know, the Supreme Court sustained its validity.

I was in court the day of that decision and, though I had a share in winning the case, it was not for me a happy day. You may ask why I did it. Of course, I could have resigned. Of course, Mr. Biddle could have resigned.

I did it because it seemed to me that the separation of function in society justified and, indeed, required the course that I pursued; that is to say that it was not my responsibility to order or not to order the Japanese evacuation, neither was it, in fact, Mr. Biddle's responsibility to do so. It was the responsibility of the President of the United States, who had been elected by the people of the United States. Neither was it either Mr. Biddle's responsibility or my responsibility to determine whether the evacuation was constitutional or not constitutional. That was the responsibility, in this context at least, of the Supreme Court of the United States, composed of nine men, nominated by a President and approved by a Senate, to hold that office.

I suggest to you, in short, that one of the ways in which a rich society avoids what might otherwise prove to be insoluble dilemmas of choice is to recognize a separation of functions, a distribution of responsibilities, with respect to problems of that kind, and this is particularly recurrent in the legal profession.

Let me carry this story somewhat further and illustrate another phase:

As you may remember, these camps were set up and many, at least, of the people who had been removed found themselves in the camps and, as you would suppose, there was grave resentment in what had been called the "Relocation Centers," and why should there not be?

But the process was undertaken of distributing the population of the camps so as to put, particularly in a camp in Northern California, at Tula Lake, those who were most dissident toward the country. At Tula Lake there were thousands of people, some families, some individuals, and by 1943 there was rioting at Tula

Lake that attracted general attention, including Congressional attention.

Investigation showed that the situation appeared to be that there were large numbers of individuals at Tula Lake who did proclaim allegiance to the Emperor of Japan, who showed this by marching and other public demonstrations designed to express that allegiance —and I'm speaking, of course, of people who were American citizens, and how much their view of their own allegiance may have been determined by the indignities to which they had been subjected only God can know, but the manifestation was there.

And so, in the spring of 1943, many members of the Congress began to press the Department of Justice very vigorously to take steps to prosecute these disloyal persons, as they were called, at Tula Lake, and there was, of course, legal ground for such prosecution.

What should Mr. Biddle's course, or mine as his Assistant, have been at that point?

In fact, proposals were made and introduced in Congress to forfeit the citizenship of persons manifesting loyalty to an enemy during the war, measures which were drafted with specific reference to these manifestations at the camp at Tula Lake.

What actually was done in the Department of Justice—and I avow large personal responsibility for this course, though you may think it wrong—was this. We considered that in this special situation individuals who, though American citizens, exhibited, felt loyalty to Japan in the war, should actually be given the opportunity to alter their citizenship, to become Japanese citizens, and then to be treated as we treated enemy aliens in the United States; that is, to be interned for the duration of the war, and then, presumably, repatriated to Japan.

This was a course that we thought to be legally possible because it was common in the Japanese situation for the person involved to hold dual citizenship; that is, Japan treated many American-Japanese as citizens of Japan—it is a common phenomenon in the history of the country—Italy did the same for many years, too.

So we proposed in Congress that the law on expatriation, which theretofore limited voluntary expatriation—that is, the renunciation of citizenship, to the case where the person renouncing was abroad —that that law should be amended to permit expatriation in the United States, requiring only that the expatriation (a) be voluntary and (b) that it be approved by the Attorney General as not contrary to the interests of national defense.

The point of the second, the national defense reservation, was that it was possible that tax evasion or other forms of legal evasion might have been involved and might have been a reason for the Attorney General not to approve this.

In any event, the Congress, somewhat desperate to know what to do in this situation, accepted that legislative proposal and the President approved the Act, and it became the law, and within a very brief time the Department of Justice received more than 5,000 requests for renunciation of citizenship, mainly from Tula Lake.

It then fell to me to undertake a program to administer this Renunciation Statute, and two courses were pressed upon me or at least two alternatives appeared. One was to take the view that we would only accept renunciation from persons whom we otherwise knew to be really loyal to Japan and not merely to have been disaffected by the evacuation. This was one course.

The other course was to read the statute as it was written and as it was meant to be read, that if the renunciation was voluntary, in the sense of not being coerced, if it was the free decision of the individual, that then it would be accepted.

And in order to determine whether it was a free decision of the individual, a hearing would be required.

I proposed, and Mr. Biddle accepted, the second course. I did so knowing that it would be likely to result in a larger number of renunciations than the first course, but I made that decision because I thought the law required it. I thought that the terms of the statute left no real room for choice.

And before writing this chapter, I took from my files a memorandum that I drew, a little later, when this matter was still fresh in my mind, in which I find that I said this:

"I have rarely been as divided in my mind and my emotions on any issue as I was on this. I thought that the alternatives"—the two I mentioned above—"were accurately posed, and that either system would be intelligible."

But then I go on, and I won't take time for the details, to say that I felt that the statute had been enacted by Congress for the express purpose of permitting those Japanese who affirmed their loyalty to Japan and, whatever the reasons, wished to be Japanese, to accomplish that purpose and thereafter be treated as enemy aliens rather than as Americans.

I mention this because some of you may have read the books on the Japanese evacuation, and I should say that the decision that I'm now mentioning has been generally condemned by all those who have written on the subject. I mean, the administrative decision.

And yet as I reflect on it again I'm sure that I would have made the same—that I would now make the same decision in the same situation, so maybe this is one of those dilemmas that the writer feels is resolved.

If there had been time, I might have mentioned two other matters that I thought might be of interest. One is the Nuremberg Trial, where, again assisting Mr. Biddle, it fell to me in the routine of office to participate in the planning for that trial.

What happened at Nuremberg, I suppose, becomes less and less popular as time goes on or, at least, if one reads the literature, the critics of the Nuremberg process far outnumber those who support it.

But, again, it would be instructive—and it's not, on the whole, what the critics do—if they should ask themselves, "What were the possibilities, as the end of the war was foreseen, what should the allied governments have done with respect to the leadership of the enemy?"

Should the position have been taken that their surrenders would be accepted and that would be the end of it? Should the position have been taken that there could be prosecutions, but only for violations of the conventional laws of war—that is, killing prisoners, and the like, as to which everyone conceded that the legal position was clear?

Should no attention have been given to what were called the "crimes against humanity"? Should no attention have been given to the question of who started the whole thing, recognizing what horrors are incident to war, inevitably, once a war has been begun?

Should the position have been taken that there would be no trials, but that individuals might be shot, and that those who could be shot would be identified by what was called in the deliberations an "executive decision"?

An executive decision—what this meant was, of course, that someone would draw up a list and the orders would go out, and the people on that list, if identified, would be shot.

These were the issues that were real in the planning of Nuremberg and I, myself, heard no less a man than Anthony Eden, at a conference in San Francisco, on this subject, state that the preference of His Majesty's Government was that there should be no trials but only executions, although the British were prepared to yield upon the point. The thought that civilized countries might have sanctioned execution without trial is one of the horrors of my recollection of that time.

I say again, the decisions that were taken may not have been right, but no critic, surely, performs the critical task unless he tells you what decision he thinks should have been made, facing the dilemmas of that time.

I've rambled, I've spoken, however, of some of the largest issues that I've had to face in my life as a lawyer. Indeed, I hope never in what remains to me of life to be confronted with such issues again. Perhaps they would illustrate the theme of this series, that for a lawyer, for a jurist, dilemmas and compromises must be the stock in trade.

XII

THE AUTHOR AND THE TRUTH[1]

BY

ELIZABETH JANEWAY

I am to speak to you on the dilemmas and compromises in the life of an author. It is, I think, an excellent subject for a writer to undertake; for all his working life is a long struggle with compromise, and with the resolution of dilemmas.

What is an author, anyway? How shall we define his work? Is he merely someone who puts words on paper, who records and reports? This he must do, of course. He must be in contact with reality— some kind of reality. He must take events as his base, whether they are physical, or emotional, or mental events. But to record events is never enough. Truth, we all know, is stranger than fiction. Truth, in fact, is incomprehensible—if by truth we mean events as they are experienced. An author cannot be content with recording events; he must also search for their meaning. Why did this happen? he must ask. What was the result? He must be an explorer of the world, and an interpreter of it.

But to be an interpreter is to be a creator. Suppose that I want —as I do, constantly—to tell you about a discovery of mine, a discovery that seems to me to explain the meaning of an event or a series of events. Then I must present this event to you so that it makes clear my discovery. I must push and pull "experience" into some kind of perspective. I must hew out the irrelevancies that entangle the nucleus of meaning, and underline its causes. I must give the external event internal form, by imposing order upon the chaos of mere experience. I must *make* something—music out of sound, sculpture out of a block of marble, a painting out of color and canvas, a book out of "what happened." A poet, in medieval Scotland, was called a "maker." And so he was, and so are all artists of any kind.

I emphasize this point, which may seem overly obvious, because it appears that people sometimes tend to think of artists as *being* something rather than as *doing* something. Artists, in this interpretation, are thought of as "Expressing themselves"; of being somehow different—and perhaps happier—than other people because their creative impulses well forth, and this makes the artist a fuller, freer person. The Portrait of the Artist as Vincent Van Gogh, and Life on the Left Bank, and Steinbeck's idylls of Cannery Row have somehow got mixed up into the oversimplified idea that to be an artist all you need is a creative personality, which allows you to lead a full life, which is a Good Thing. Well, of course, artists have an urge to create—but it is not an urge in a vacuum. It is an urge to create *something*. It is an urge to take hold of the material of life and wrestle it into some kind of shape. Without the material, the urge is meaningless. Without the product, the artist is only a restless and frustrated human being.

I run into a certain number of people who want to write, and usually it seems as if they wanted to write in the way one wants to scratch where it itches. If they think of the products of writing at all, it is as enhancements to their personalities. "It must be wonderful to be able to write," they say wistfully. "Tell me—how long does it take to write a book?" I have given up asking what kind of a book by now; and since I can truthfully say that it took me seven years to write my first novel, I tell them this; and then they usually go away and trouble me no more. They are often nice people and I do not want to sound mean about them—but they have got hold of the wrong end of the stick. Being a writer seems the important thing to them, and writing a delightful way of expressing one's personality and relieving inner tensions. The books they think of last, as mere byproducts of personal expression.

This is a complete inversion of the truth. Actually the books come first. What is important is the product. The process, the writing, is important only because of what it produces. The writer as a person isn't important at all. He's an instrument for the production of books. The personal satisfaction he gets out of it doesn't matter any more than the satisfaction one gets out of playing a good game of tennis. A writer is a maker, and he must never, never forget that what matters is what he makes.

Why have I gone into all this definition? Because the dilemmas of a writer are the dilemmas of someone who is making something and must think first of his product. It may seem odd, but they are really not internal dilemmas at all. They have little to do with a writer's character—unless he's lazy and doesn't work as hard as he should. But when he *is* working, he's concerned with choices that are quite external to his personal life, and lie between him and his material. *In his work,* he doesn't have to worry about how to win friends and influence people, nor does he have to suppress his opinions in order to hold a job.

I am of course speaking now of novelists. If you are writing political articles for a newspaper with a decided political bias, you may well run the risk of having them rejected if you express opinions diametrically opposed to the policy of the editors. I assume that any-one who writes political articles has the sense to know this—but I would also add that a good article, rooted in fact, will very often be published even when it does point away from the aim of the medium in which it appears.

To return to the novelist and his dilemmas: I will give you one more example of what he need *not* worry about. He need not worry about compromising his artistic integrity for the sake of commercial success. In the first place, it is quite possible for commercial success to come to good, serious writers. But in any case, it is achieved, ninety-nine per cent of the time, by people whose artistic integrity directs them to write that way. As for the other one per cent—it is just possible, very occasionally, to write down to an audience you despise and succeed in pleasing it. But the effort involved is so enormous and the chances of failure so large that it really isn't worth the trouble. Those historical novels, I assure you, are written by people who enjoy writing them and find their products thoroughly satisfactory.

The dilemma that faces an author, in other words, is not a moral one. It is an esthetic one. It is how to make clear what he wants to say, how to reconcile his vision and his own abilities. It is in part, therefore, a technical problem in communication, such as every human being faces, since every human being is a member of society and must communicate with his fellows. How can I move you? How can I persuade you and convince you that what I say about the world is true? That is the technical problem that the author faces in constructing a product that will show forth his discovery.

But before we come to the communication of the author's discovery, we have another problem to deal with. No one can describe what he has felt, or seen, or thought, unless he is clear about what it is he has felt or seen or thought. You have to know what you want to say in order to say it. A good deal of muddled writing is the result *not* of poor communication but of unclear vision. Concerned with events an author must certainly be, for events are the only material he has to work with. But it must be a concern as cold and objective and impartial as the scientist's. When I have failed with a character or a situation, it is almost always, I have found, because I have an emotional involvement with the character or the action which prevents me from seeing it clearly. To get it right, I have to detach myself from it.

My own method of doing this may perhaps be of interest. It's really a very simple one. I put the action that I want to see better up on a stage, and I go and sit down in the auditorium and watch it. It is happening up there—but I am separated from it by the footlights and several rows of empty seats in front of me. I don't attempt to judge or criticise or edit—not then. I just watch. When I can see it, when I can hear the voices, I put down what is said and done. As long as I can see it clearly, what I put down will be right. When my vision begins to waver and the voices fade out, I must stop— or I will begin to make things up.

I agree that this is all fantasy. Of course, I make it all up. I don't take notes on the conversation of my friends and family or record the events of the day in a journal and refer earnestly back to them when I want a touch of realism. It all comes out of my head. But I assure you that there is a very different feeling about seeing a story happen without one's apparent volition, and consciously "Making something up." In the first instance, my material and I are cooperating at a very deep level of interaction, where intuitive knowledge can supplement conscious inquiry. *I am being used by the material.* The truth that is in it is finding a road to communication through me. But in the second instance, I am merely using my material. I am unable to listen to what it has to say. I am telling it what it wants to do, instead of letting it tell me what it wants to do. And it—the material—always knows better than I. I can't tell it the truth, but it can tell me—if I listen.

For this is at once the major dilemma and the vital aim of the writer—how to tell the truth. I repeat that this is not a moral problem. The writer is not concerned with what is good. He is concerned with what is true. If he falsifies the truth and pushes his characters around for the sake of principle—even the highest principle—he is faking, just as a scientist who "cooks" an experiment is faking. Besides, he will have an unconvincing book on his hands.

Now of course authors write about morals. They write about them I guess, more than about anything else. But that is because morals are a very important part of human society. There have certainly been many moving books written that uphold a moral principle—that intolerance is a bad thing, for instance. But when you examine them, why was *Uncle Tom's Cabin* a moving book? Or *Strange Fruit?* Or *Cry the Beloved Country? Not* because of the moral content in them. They moved their readers to tears and to anger because in each case the author was able to convince his audience that he had discovered, in reality, the truth about *why* intolerance is a bad thing. He did not depend upon the statement of a moral principle, but went humbly to experience to ask it to show him the truth about what he believed. He had been convinced that he had made a discovery about the world, and his concern was to order his material according to its own laws so that his discovery could shine through. In so far as his book was successful, he was not a missionary stating an *a priori* truth, but an interpreter explaining an empirical truth.

Of course, the viewpoint from which we gaze upon truth changes as the times change. Today we are apt to find Alan Paton's interpretation more convincing than Harriet Beecher Stowe's. But that is only to say that we naturally find it easier to recognize a truth when the unspoken assumptions of our own time are taken into account.

What is truth? I will leave Pilate's question up to you. Nor do I know whether truth is eternal. Because the writer is a maker, and a doer, he can be content with a relative truth, one that rings true when he tests it against his experience. Some truths are bigger than others, and their importance endures longer and is of greater concern to more people than others. But if a writer has got hold of a truth, even a small one, he will do well to listen to it. Truth is not his weapon. Even the smallest truth is too big for that. The writer is the instrument of the truth, not the other way round.

So we have the writer clutching his discovery, clutching his truth. It is a relative truth, and it is not quite the same as any other writer's, for naturally we see most clearly what our interests and character and intelligence and experience fit us to see. But still, we must see, we must have our vision. Here there is no room for compromise. Then, however, the writer faces the long struggle to set down on paper what he has seen, and here there is always compromise, for no one can ever write as clearly, as movingly, as vividly as he hopes to. How delighted I have been sometimes with something I have written! How good it seems as I write it, while the vision of what I want to write still shimmers behind it! And afterwards —well, afterwards how thin and pedestrian it sometimes seems. I have done my best—but it is never good enough!

No one more than the writer has ground into him the fundamental fact that compromise is an essential part of life. You are familiar, no doubt, with Sigmund Freud's famous conception of the "omnipotence of thought"—or it might be called "the omnipotence of wishes." In dreams, said Freud, and in certain forms of insanity, the individual is convinced that all he has to do, to make something happen, is to wish for it to happen. Freud held that primitive belief in magic is an example of this ancient and universal tendency. Well, the writer, of all people, has a chance to try out the omnipotence of his thought. He has merely to conceive of something happening, you might think, in order to have it happen in his books.

But between the magic of the beginning and the finished book —so many pages, published by Thus and So, Incorporated, $3.50 a copy—comes the long anguish and joy of—compromise. For in order to bring your situation to life, to make it more than a private symbol, you must bathe it in the right atmosphere, people it with the characters who will act as you desire them to. Let's take an obvious wish-situation. Suppose that you—the writer—have been disappointed in love. You want to write a book in which you get the girl, instead of your hated rival. Do you imagine it's easy? Oh dear, oh dear, think what you have to do! In order to make what went wrong come right, you have to change one of the three main characters— yourself, the girl, or the rival. To change the character convincingly, you must understand it. So you have to plumb the depths of your own soul, or the one you love, or the one you hate, or very likely all three. Then when you think you know what to do, you have to write about things so close to you emotionally that you look a bit cross-eyed at them. You have to take the wish that started you out on all this and put it in harness, use it to create not a dream world, but a world so real, so recognizable, that your readers will feel at home in it. Do you think for a moment you can do that without compromising every step of the way? By the time you get through, if you've got a book worth talking about, you've probably changed yourself and the girl and the rival into quite different people—or awarded her to him with a paean of thanksgiving. In any case, the "omnipotence of thought" has been modified by the demands of creating a convincing situation as much as if it had been tested by action in the real world instead of by literary creation.

I have never, myself, felt that I was writing a book in order to make a wish come true—except the wish to write a book. This is no doubt an important wish—but important only to me, as a person, and not important at all to the finished book. It's not the wish, but the work that makes a book. It's true that the wish makes the beginning easy—or at any rate, makes the beginning fun. I begin by being haunted. A character pops up and possesses me, real as a hallucination, demanding as an angry ghost. "You must write about me!" cries Nina Bishop or Lydia Walsh or John Gregory or Daisy Kenyon. "Let me tell you my troubles, and you'll see why I need a book." If you want to tell me that Nina or Lydia is a slightly neurotic projection of part of myself, that's all right with me. I don't mind. The main thing is that she's there, to hold my hand and lead me on and babble in my ear and get me started.

Then, somewhere along the line, my friendly ghost vanishes. Things aren't so easy now. I'm left alone to gaze at empty pages until I'm almost afraid to begin to cover them; or worse, with scribbled pages that I'm sure are wrong and must be thrown away. And I sit and I stare and insidiously there creeps into my mind the thought of some necessary household task, neglected now for days, that I might be doing instead. So much *easier* to stop now and go weed the flower beds and wait for inspiration. So much more important to dash out and buy the laundry basket and the carving knife and the tan shoe polish that I've forgotten to get, than to sit and sit like a broody hen on an egg that refuses to hatch. But inspiration won't do it and magic won't do it, and thought is not omnipotent at all. I have to make something. I have to go back to the material—read over the story, listen to it, begin to hear again, invoke not the ghost but the shadowy structure of the finished book, wait and work and make a false start and finally, haltingly, get under way once more. And so on and on, between vision and practice, until I compromise my way to the end. If I have done anything worth doing, written anything worth reading, I have managed to set down something that is true about how people behave, I have made it understandable to my readers, and I have cast it in a shape that has its own unity and form.

Which is the most important—to see the truth, to communicate the truth, or to do it with beauty and grace and unity? On different levels, each is the most important. How magnificently a great writer does all three! Think of *War and Peace*. It is impossible to say which aspect of this wonderful book we admire most—whether it is the profound truths of human behavior that Tolstoy saw, or the unforgettable scenes in which he presented them or the sweep and power of the book itself. Each is present, modifying and heightening the others. Do we not see in such a work the positive virtues of compromise? Vision and reality have done more than blend. Compromise has become the synthesis that produces something new and formative.

Evolutionists tell us that the forms of life which have survived in nature are the forms which have been unspecialized. To adapt *too* well to any one set of circumstances is to mark oneself for extinction. The specialized dinosaurs died out while the humble little nocturnal creatures that became the mammals lived on, because they were able to change as the external situation changed. Those who could compromise lived. Those who could not died.

On the level of mere survival, then, we find that the ability to compromise, to resolve dilemmas in a new way, is a life-giving force. It seems to me that our great writers—let me say again, our great "makers"—serve the rest of humanity in just this way. Shakespeare and Goethe, Tolstoy and Dickens, Melville and Faulkner, are the explorers, the frontiersmen of society. The problems that confuse and muddle the rest of us sweep over them, too. But where *we* are reduced to despair or to impotence, the great writer seizes upon the dilemmas facing his times as challenges and opportunities. He does not just *wish* to solve them, and "make up" a solution. He actively tries to solve them. He goes down and down and down into them, seeking for their deepest meaning. He must take nothing for granted. Because he is looking for truth, he must be willing to shatter old definitions of truth. Many will find this shocking. They will call him an iconoclast. And so in a way, he is. But no definition of truth contains the whole of truth. What is true will renew itself in a fresh definition. And it is the makers who give us these definitions.

But now we come to an odd thing. We find that our greatest writers resort to fiction in order to tell the truth. Why should this be? If you grant me that great fiction is a special kind of truth, you may still wonder at it. Is it because we, the audience, are such babies that we must have truth sugarcoated with a story if we are to swallow it? Well yes, it is, in part. We do like exciting narrative, we are more easily convinced by the words of a sympathetic character than by a didactic statement. Naturally the writer takes advantages of these aids to persuasion.

There is another reason, however, for the use of fiction to impart truth. Truth is elusive and delicate and complicated. Words are clumsy. Indeed, words themselves are compromises—they have to cover so many situations that they can never mean just one thing. Philosophers attempt to make words take on a unitary meaning by going through a lengthy process of definition—and then they end, usually (unless they are also poets and makers) by writing a private jargon. No, words are too coarse a mesh to be used to *tell* truth, straight out.

So the writer attempts to *show* the truth. He creates a fictional situation which corresponds (he believes) to the reality he has discovered. Bit by bit, as the action of the story progresses, we come to see what he is driving at. He sets up the structure of his book as an example of truth. Yes, it is something he has made up—but he has made it up this way and no other because in this way it shows us what he has discovered about reality. A good book is not the fulfillment of an arbitrary personal wish. It is a window on the world.

May I make a confession? I said that as the story grows, the reader comes to see what the writer is driving at. Well, sometimes it is only as the story grows that the writer comes to see, himself, what he is driving at. I have always been fond of the old lady who, when told to think before she spoke, replied: "How do I know what I think until I hear what I say?" I sympathize with her deeply, for I have never been entirely sure what I am going to write until the material tells me as I write it. Once, indeed, I made an outline for a book—it was for the second draft of my first novel. I was learning to write a novel, you see, and I was determined to be professional about it. Well, as I finished each chapter I discovered that the outline had to be changed. Something had happened, each time, that I hadn't foreseen. I changed that outline doggedly eight times. Right down to the last chapter my material defied me. I wished Lydia Walsh to marry. I was wrong. I bullied Lydia in my mind ahead of time, but when it came right down to it, she wouldn't get married and I couldn't make her. So I gave up, and I have never made another outline. Nowadays I wait to see what I say before I decide what I think.

Isn't that pretty chancy? you may ask. How can you possibly claim you've laid hold of any kind of truth, even the smallest, if you don't know what it is ahead of time? The answer is: How can I tell if it's true until I test it? And I have to test it in the writing. For me, the discovery and communication of truth and the shaping of it into the form that expresses it best are all compounded together. And I believe that what is true for me, on my small scale, is true for the great writers on their much grander scale. Writing is a process of analysis and synthesis, and the two are so intermingled that they can never be entirely separated.

Perhaps this is the most creative compromise of all. For it is just here that creation takes place and the new thing is made, here where the writer reacts to his material, where he sees and says, where what is true speaks through him as an instrument. It is a slow process, making anything, and making it, moreover, in the shape that its own inner laws demand. In a world where most things are made by machines, and plastics can be stamped out in any form at all, it is rather a strange thing to be doing. You, who work with people, and who know that important human relationships are also plants of slow growth, will understand why I value the feeling of process that is part of making a book.

I like that word—process. It is close to the word you asked me to talk about—compromise. In the process of making a book, the arrogance of the maker must be blended with the humility of the seeker for truth. The conscious will must learn that it can subdue stubborn reality only when it understands the inner form of reality. The impatience of the dreamer must come down to earth and plug along at daily routine. One can't always be writing big scenes any more than one can always be living them—people have to open doors and talk about the weather in books, too. One must be even more careful about one's emotions—for a writer infatuated with his hero will produce not a hero, but a block of wood—careful about prejudices, too. A writer has them, of course, but when they get into a book, they deaden it. In short, one must learn that in the very process of making something peculiarly one's own—one must not impose oneself upon it, but forget oneself. To make a book is to make something with a life of its own, that in the end doesn't belong to the writer at all, but to everyone in the world who is reached and moved by it. It is a contribution to our common heritage of culture, which is the only thing that makes us human at all.

I haven't said anything very new, I'm afraid, but I have at least tried to practice what I preach, and to say only what I believe to be true. So I repeat, to us who are always facing the dilemma of creation, who tell the truth by way of fiction, who must let the characters we "make up" construct our story for us, who are patient and impatient, humble and arrogant, who don't know what we think till we see what we say—for us, compromise does not mean defeat or confusion. It means the marriage of opposites and the birth of something new from the marriage. It means insight into diversity. It means the way we do our work.

CONTRIBUTORS TO "INTEGRITY AND COMPROMISE: PROBLEMS OF PUBLIC AND PRIVATE CONSCIENCE" *

FRANCIS BIDDLE, LL.D., Boston University, etc.; Former Attorney General of the United States; Author, *Llanfear Pattern, Mr. Justice Holmes, Democratic Thinking and the War, The World's Best Hope, The Fear of Freedom.*

EUGENE EXMAN, M.A., The University of Chicago, D. Rel. Ed., *h.c.;* Director and Vice-President of Harper & Brothers and Manager of its religious book department.

ELIZABETH JANEWAY, A.B., Barnard College; Author, *The Walsh Girls, Daisy Kenyon, The Question of Gregory, The Vikings, Leaving Home.*

JOHN LAFARGE, S.J., B.A., Harvard University, M.A., Woodstock College; Associate Editor, *"America";* Author, *Jesuits in Modern Times, Interracial Justice, The Race Question and the Negro, No Postponement, L'Homme de Couleur, The Manner Is Ordinary.*

DOROTHY D. LEE, Ph.D., University of California; Consultant in Teaching and Program Leader in Anthropology, The Merrill-Palmer School, Detroit.

R. M. MACIVER, D. Phil., Edinburgh University, D. Litt., Columbia University, Harvard University; Lieber Professor Emeritus of Political Philosophy and Sociology, Columbia University; Vice President, Conference on Science, Philosophy and Religion; Member, Executive Committee, The Institute for Religious and Social Studies; Author, *The Pursuit of Happiness, The Web of Government, The More Perfect Union, The Ramparts We Guard, Democracy and the Economic Challenge,* and others; Editor, *Group Relations and Group Antagonisms, Civilization and Group Relationships, Unity and Difference in American Life, Discrimination and National Welfare, Great Expressions of Human Rights, Conflict of Loyalties, Moments of Personal Discovery, The Hour of Insight, New Horizons in Creative Thinking: A Survey and Forecast, Great Moral Dilemmas: In Literature, Past and Present;*

* As of October, 1955.

Co-Editor: Symposia of the Conference on Science, Philosophy and Religion.

JULIUS MARK, Rabbi, D.D., Hebrew Union College, etc.; Senior Rabbi, Congregation Emanu-El; Author, *Behaviorism and Religion.*

EUGENE J. McCARTHY, M.A., University of Minnesota; Former Acting Chairman, Department of Sociology, St. Thomas College; Representative from Minnesota, United States House of Representatives; Member, Committee on Ways and Means.

GEORGE L. K. MORRIS, A.B., Yale University; Former President, American Abstract Artists; painter and sculptor.

PETER MARSHALL MURRAY, M.D., Howard University; Director, Obstetrics and Gynecology, Sydenham Hospital.

ALBERT J. PENNER, B.D., Hartford Theological Seminary; Minister, The Broadway Congregational Church.

I. I. RABI, Ph.D., Columbia University, etc.; Higgins Professor of Physics, Columbia University.

HERBERT WECHSLER, A.B., City College of New York, LL.B., Columbia University; Professor of Law, Columbia University; Author, *Criminal Law and Its Administration* (with J. Michael), *The Federal Courts and the Federal System* (with H. Hart, Jr.).

INDEX

Patience:
defined, 15
vs. sacred zeal, 15
Paton, Alan, 121-122
Pauling, Linus, 39
Penner, Albert J., 43-53
Physician, dilemmas and compromises encountered by, 55-63
Pilate, Pontius, 134
Planned Parenthood, dilemma caused by, 48
Plastic arts, 97
Political compromise, four categories of, 22
Politician:
as compromiser, 19
as moralist, 28
Politics:
compromise and, 6, 19-28
one definition of, 19
Portrait painters, and art values, 94
Prayer, 68
Presbyterian Church, 44
see also Protestant churches
Priesthood, compromise and, 9-17
Private enterprise, absence of, among Hopi Indians, 88
Propaganda, 113
Prophetic preaching by rabbis, 74
Prophets, Hebrew, compared with present-day rabbis, 67
Prosperity, as sign of divine favor in Bible, 41
Protestant-Catholic-Jew, 46
Protestant-Catholic marriages, 53
Protestant churches:
competition among, 44-45
growing memberships of, 45
money-raising schemes of, 45
Protestant minister:
dilemmas and compromises in work of, 43-45
economic security and social needs of, 44
leadership vs. limited authority of, 50
priestly vs. prophetic functions of, 49

Pueblo Indians, 84
Pulpit, as platform for free speech, 49

Rabbi:
compared with ancient prophets, 67
compromise on ritual by, 71
dilemmas encountered by, 65
limited time for scholarship by, 69
prophetic preaching by, 74
social and community activities of, 70
Rabi, I. I., 29-41
biographical details, 31
Race question, compromise on, 26
Race relations, community problems and, 13
Racial antagonism, in foreign affairs, 27
Racial discrimination, 10
Radar, development of, 32
Radiation laboratory, M.I.T., 32
Reform, social, confused ideas of, 14
Reform rabbi, 71
Relative, vs. absolute, 4
Relative truth, 134
Religion:
ageing and, 39-40
totality of, in Jewish view, 69
Religious insight, and vocational dilemma, 107
Renunciation Statute, and Japanese aliens in U.S., 126-127
Republican party, differences with Democratic party, 3, 21
Research, scientific, 30
Revolutionary War, Burke's compromise plea and, 65
Ritual, Jewish, 71
"Ritualistic liberals," 14
Roosevelt, Eleanor, 98
Rosenberg spy case, 48
Rosh Hashonah, 71
Russia, atomic energy developments of, 37-38

Sacred zeal, defined, 15
Salesman, dilemmas of, 114
Sanger, Margaret, 48
Saturday Evening Post, 93